A Glossary
of
Liturgical
Terms

Dennis C. Smolarski, SJ
with Joseph DeGrocco

LTP
LITURGY
TRAINING
PUBLICATIONS

Nihil Obstat
Very Reverend Daniel A. Smilanic, JCD
Vicar for Canonical Services
Archdiocese of Chicago
May 22, 2017

Imprimatur
Very Reverend Ronald A. Hicks
Vicar General
Archdiocese of Chicago
May 22, 2017

A GLOSSARY OF LITURGICAL TERMS © 2017 Archdiocese of Chicago: Liturgy Training Publications, 3949 South Racine Avenue, Chicago, IL 60609; 800-933-1800; fax 800-933-7094; e-mail: orders@ltp.org; website: www.LTP.org. All rights reserved.

This book was edited by Victoria M. Tufano. Christian Rocha was the production editor, Juan Alberto Castillo was the designer, and Luis Leal was the production artist.

Art by Martin Erspamer, OSB.

21 20 19 18 17   1 2 3 4 5

Printed in the United States of America.

Library of Congress Control Number: 2017948551

ISBN 978-1-61671-361-4

GLT

A Glossary of Liturgical Terms

INTRODUCTION

In 1987, Eric D. Hirsch Jr. published his somewhat controversial book *Cultural Literacy*, in which he suggested that literacy goes beyond merely being able to read and write. Hirsch proposed that contemporary Americans should be exposed to a body of knowledge in order to appreciate the achievements of the past and make similar progress for the future. The exposure to a body of knowledge would enable individuals to recognize significant words, phrases, and allusions, particularly in texts or speeches, which they might otherwise not recognize. As one example, Hirsch pointed out that many of the biblical and religious phrases and the allusions to the Declaration of Independence and other documents of US civic culture that were included in Martin Luther King's famous "I have a dream" speech were less and less recognizable to younger Americans in the late 1980s.

To remedy this "cultural illiteracy," Hirsch also included a proposed "literacy list" in his original book, and it was that list that was the source of controversy, since there were reactions as to why certain items were included in the list and others not. Within a year, Hirsch published a revised "literacy list" in the paperback edition of his book and also published *The Dictionary of Cultural Literacy: What Every American Needs to Know* with coauthors Joseph F. Kett and James Trefil in 1988 (which has subsequently been revised several times).

The Catholic Church has its own culture and a specialized vocabulary, including words particularly used in its liturgical life. After reading Hirsch's book in 1987, I authored the book *Liturgical*

Literacy: From Anamnesis to Worship (Paulist Press, 1990), which contained over 650 entries with definitions, in an attempt to gather into one volume the terms commonly used to describe liturgical objects and activities. I also included dates and names of important events, individuals, and documents related to the Catholic liturgical tradition.

This volume builds on the earlier book, which has been out of print for many years. It includes many of the original entries, omits some entries, and adds others. All the definitions have been reviewed, and some have been revised or expanded.

Why might such a collection of liturgical terms and their definitions be useful at this point of history? The contemporary American Catholic Church is much more diverse than that of the decades prior to the Second Vatican Council, and the background of American Catholics is far from being as homogeneous as it once was. In the 1950s and 1960s, many Catholics came from a European background, had been educated in a parochial school (as were their parents), and had learned a religious vocabulary through common religious texts, particularly the American *Baltimore Catechism.* Many Catholics of that generation were taught the names of the sacraments, vestments, and altar appointments and participated in various devotions and processions that were a regular part of parish life. But the face of American Catholicism has changed significantly over the last half century. Fewer children are enrolled in parochial schools, and more parishes are becoming more ethnically diverse as new immigrants arrive, most often from countries other than those of Europe, often to escape hardship and even persecution in the lands of their birth. In addition, matters pertaining to religious education, liturgical planning, and marriage preparation, areas which once were the almost exclusive domain of the parish priests and the religious women and men who taught in schools in many parishes, have now become the responsibility of lay women and men.

Some of the many dedicated lay women and men who are involved in parish life (for example as directors of religious education) have been trained in intensive programs in theology, spirituality, or catechetics and have earned graduate degrees or some sort of certification—such individuals usually know most of the standard liturgical terms. Others (for example, volunteer sacristans, coordinators of extraordinary ministers of Holy Communion, or ministers to the sick and homebound) may be dedicated individuals who have participated for decades in the liturgical life of their parish, but have less formal training in religious areas—such individuals often learn new terms as needed in their ministry. Still others, trained decades ago in religious matters yet involved in nonreligious fields for years, may have not used technical words associated with the liturgical life of the Church for quite a while—such individuals may need to refresh their memory if they should become more involved in one way or another in the liturgical or ministerial life of the parish.

This book is meant to help all individuals who are involved in the liturgical life of their parish or who are involved in the education of the youth or adults of the parish. Just as we need a standard vocabulary to express ourselves about the various aspects of our secular lives, whether those aspects pertain to politics, entertainment, sports, industry, automobiles, environment, weather, or family life, so too we need to know the words and terms commonly used in our liturgical life, which, by far, is the aspect of Church life that touches Catholics most frequently and (dare I say) most deeply. It is helpful to know the difference between a chasuble and a dalmatic, between an alb and a surplice, between a corporal and a purificator. Hence, the utility of a book that contains the major special terms related to the liturgical life of the Church.

Of course, it is one thing to have a list of words, phrases, names, and titles, as well as their definitions. But it is a far different thing to use these words, phrases, names, and titles in a coherent fashion. And even more importantly, it is much more significant to realize that the reality behind the words, phrases, names, and titles contained in this book points to a reality that is beyond all words: the mystery of God the Father and his love incarnate in Jesus, his Son, who both send the Spirit to enliven and sanctify us on our journey toward the new and eternal Jerusalem.

Projects such as this book are, in this present age, never the result of one person working alone. Many people have been involved to produce this current volume. Particular thanks go to the staff at Liturgy Training Publications, particularly Lorie Simmons, who contacted me years ago about the project, and Vicky Tufano, who has seen it to its completion. Much thanks also goes to Msgr. Joseph DeGrocco of the diocese of Rockville Center for his insight and energy in reviewing the list of entries and who suggested additions, deletions, and emendations to definitions.

Words are needed to describe important realities and we must never forget that Jesus is the Word who "became flesh and dwelt among us." But so often words do fail us when trying to describe what is of ultimate importance—our relationship with God and with others in the Christian community.

Dennis C. Smolarski, SJ
July 2016

Editor's note: Words that appear in boldface in a definition also have their own entries in this book.

Ablution   A term previously used for the cleansing of the vessels after **Holy Communion,** particularly the **chalice**. This cleansing is now referred to as the **purification**.

Ablution Bowl   A small vessel of **water**, usually with a cover, kept near the **tabernacle**. It is used by **ministers** to cleanse their fingers after distributing **Holy Communion**. It is also called an *ablution* cup.

Absolution   A text declaring or requesting from God the forgiveness of sins.

In the **Sacrament** of **Penance,** the sacramental forgiveness of sins is obtained from God through the solemn declaration of the **priest**. This declaration constitutes the **form** of the sacrament and is spoken by the priest while he extends his hand(s) over the head of the **penitent**.

In the **Mass,** the words that conclude the **penitential act,** "May almighty God have mercy on us, forgive us our sins, and bring us to everlasting life," are called an absolution, but they are not considered sacramental in effect.

Abstinence   Refraining from eating a certain type of food. Roman Catholic custom prescribes that, in general, Ash Wednesday and all Fridays are days of abstinence from meat. In the United States, Catholics are required to abstain from meat on **Ash Wednesday,** onthe Fridays of **Lent,** and on **Good Friday**.

Accidents   The external appearances of physical **matter**. It is a classical philosophical term used in contrast to the term **substance**. This distinction provides the basis for the term **transubstantiation**, an explanation of how **bread** and **wine** become the Body and Blood of **Christ**. In the Eucharist, the accidents of bread and wine (for example, the taste and the aroma) remain while the substance of each is transformed.

Acclamation   A brief, joyful liturgical response, such as "**Amen**" or "Blessed be God!"

Acolyte   The liturgical **minister** charged with assisting the **priest** and **deacon** in the **sanctuary**. Although the title is frequently applied to any **altar server**, *acolyte* more specifically refers to one who has been instituted in this ministry through the liturgical **rite** called the **Institution** of Acolytes, which is **celebrated** almost exclusively for men preparing for **ordination**.

Act of Contrition   A traditional Catholic prayer expressing sorrow for sin and resolution not to sin again. This prayer is often used as the **prayer of the penitent** in the **Sacrament** of **Penance**, although other expressions of sorrow are also appropriate.

Act of Penance   An act of **satisfaction**, or atonement, imposed on the **penitent** by the **priest** as part of the **Sacrament** of **Penance**. It is meant to be a remedy for sin and a help in changing one's life, and should include amends for any injury done to others, if appropriate. The **penance** imposed should in some way correspond to the sin and might include prayer, self-denial, or some work of service or mercy toward another person.

Active Participation   Engagement in and attentiveness to the liturgical actions which are being **celebrated**. Achieving the "full, conscious, and active" participation of all the faithful, according to the *Constitution on the Sacred Liturgy* (no. 14), was the goal of the liturgical reforms following the Second Vatican Council. The word *active* denotes not only physical activity, but also attentive listening and focused **silence** at appropriate times. Thus, full, conscious, and active participation involves both interior and exterior aspects of human engagement.

Ad Orientem   **Latin** phrase meaning "to the east." It describes the celebration of **Mass** in which the **priest** and the people face in the same direction. The direction is presumed to be east, the direction of the rising sun and, according to tradition, the direction from which **Christ** will return at the end of time. Whether it is in fact east or not depends on the direction that the **church** building faces.

Adoration, Eucharistic   The practice of prayer before the **Blessed Sacrament**. The practice stems from the Catholic belief that **Christ** remains truly present in the **consecrated bread** and **wine** even after the conclusion of the **Mass**.

Adult   For the purpose of sacramental initiation, a person who reaches the age of reason (also called the age of discretion or **catechetical age**), usually regarded to be seven years of age, is an adult. A person who has reached that age is to be initiated into the **Church** according to the *Rite of Christian Initiation of Adults* and receive all three **sacraments of initiation** together, although the catechesis should be adapted to their needs. Before this age, the person is considered an infant and is baptized using the *Rite of Baptism for Children*.

Advent   The liturgical **time** of joyful preparation and anticipation for **Christmas**. It is also a time of **penance**, although this aspect is secondary to the spirit of hope-filled waiting. This time, considered to be the start of a new **liturgical year**, begins on the fourth **Sunday** before Christmas.

Affusion   The method of administering **Baptism** by which the **minister** pours **water** over the head of the **candidate** while pronouncing the baptismal formula. Although affusion is probably the most common way of administering the sacrament in the **Latin Church**, Baptism by **immersion** (also called **infusion**) is preferred because of its fuller symbolism.

Agape   Greek word for love, specifically selfless love that seeks nothing other than the good of the beloved, with nothing sought in return; 1 Corinthians 13 expresses this kind of love. It is also the term used to denote a meal, or "love feast," sometimes held by the early **Church** in connection with a Eucharistic celebration.

Agnus Dei   Latin for "**Lamb of God.**" It usually refers to the **invocation** sung or spoken as the Eucharistic **Bread** is broken by the priest. It is sometimes used as the name for this **ritual** act, formally called the **fraction of the Bread**.

Alb   A full-length white liturgical robe, from the **Latin** *albus*, meaning white. The alb is the preferred vestment for all **ministers**, from **server** to **bishop**. It recalls the **white garment** put on at **Baptism** as a **sign** of putting on the new life of **Christ**. **Ordained** ministers wear a **stole** and an outer garment over the alb.

Alleluia   Hebrew for "Praise the **Lord**"; an **acclamation** of praise. It is found in the Old Testament, particularly the psalms. In some translations of the **Bible** it is found as "Hallelujah" or "Praise the Lord." In Roman Catholic **liturgy** it is used especially during **Easter Time** and omitted during **Lent**. At **Mass** it is sung before the proclamation of the **Gospel**.

Altar   The sacred table on which the **sacrifice** of the **Mass** is celebrated. It is the central **symbol** of **Christ** in a **church** building. In the United States, the table of the altar may be made of stone or wood; the base or supports may be made of any dignified and solid material. In new churches there is to be only one altar.

Altar Cloth   The cloth used to cover the **altar** during the celebration of **Mass**. One white cloth is required; additional cloths of other festive colors may be used, provided the uppermost cloth covering the top of the altar is **white**.

Altar Cross   A cross with the figure of the crucified **Christ** on or near the **altar** during the celebration of **Mass**. If the **processional cross** bears a figure of the crucified Christ, it may serve as the altar cross.

Altar of Repose   The **altar** to which the **Blessed Sacrament** is carried in **procession** and on which it is reserved at the conclusion of the **Evening Mass of the Lord's Supper** on **Holy Thursday**.

Altar Server   The liturgical **minister** who assists the **priest** and **deacon** at liturgies.

Ambo   The place from which all the Scripture readings are **proclaimed** and the **homily** may be preached during **liturgy**; a **pulpit** or **lectern**. The ambo is also used for the singing of the **Exsultet**, for announcing the **intentions** of the **Universal Prayer**, and for the leading of the **responsorial psalm**. The term is derived from a Greek word for "raised place."

Ambry   A place for the storing of the **holy oils** (chrism, **oil of catechumens**, and **oil of the sick**). In older **churches** the ambry was a niche in the wall, often with a locking door. In new and renovated churches, the ambry is often located near the **baptismal font** and constructed so that the vessels containing the holy oils can be seen. It is also spelled *aumbry*.

Amen   Hebrew word meaning "so be it." It is a response of the **assembly** indicating agreement or assent. The Great Amen is the concluding **acclamation** to the **Eucharistic Prayer**.

Amice   A **vestment** consisting of a white linen cloth, approximately two feet by three feet in size, with tie ribbons. It is worn under the **alb**, draped over the shoulders and tied around the chest. The top is tucked into the collar so that street clothing does not show at the neck line of the alb.

Anamnesis   A concept similar to *remembrance* and **memorial**, in which an event is recalled not only as a past occurrence but also, and more importantly, as a present and effective saving reality. It is a Greek word derived from the verb "to remember."

All Christian **worship** is fundamentally anamnesis. It recalls, celebrates, and makes present and effective the salvation brought about by the death and Resurrection of Jesus. *Anamnesis* is the word used in **Christ's** command at the **Last Supper**, "Do this in memory of me" (Luke 22:19).

The term also refers to a specific element in the **Eucharistic Prayer**, following the **Institution Narrative**, which explicitly remembers Christ's Death and Resurrection while making a statement of offering.

Anaphora   Greek term derived from the verb "to offer." In Greek-speaking **churches** it is the term used for the **Eucharistic Prayer**.

Angels   Pure spirits created by God who offer God praise and adoration and are sent by God as messengers. Tradition offers specific names for nine **orders**, or **choirs**, of angels: angels, **archangels**, virtues, powers, principalities, dominions, thrones, cherubim, and **seraphim**. During **Mass**, the **preface** declares that the **worshiping assembly** joins with the angels in praising God in the singing of the **Holy, Holy, Holy**.

Anoint   To apply oil as part of a liturgical **rite**. Anointing with oil takes place in the **Baptism** of infants, in the **Anointing of the Catechumens**, in the **Sacrament** of **Confirmation**, in the **Anointing of the Sick**, in the **ordination** of **bishops** and **priests**, and in the dedication of **churches** and **altars**.

Anointing of the Catechumens   One of the **rites** that takes place during the period of the **catechumenate**. Catechumens are **anointed** by a **priest** or **deacon** with the **oil of catechumens** whenever it seems beneficial or desirable to do so, to symbolize their need and desire for God's help and strength.

Anointing of the Sick   The **sacrament** of healing for seriously ill individuals. Those whose health is seriously impaired by physical or mental sickness or age and request this sacrament are **anointed** with the **oil of the sick** so that they may be spiritually strengthened in their afflictions by **Christ**, who throughout his ministry healed those with various afflictions. It finds its biblical basis in James 5:14, which describes **priests** of the **Church** praying over the sick and anointing them. Before the Second Vatican Council, this sacrament was known as **Extreme Unction**.

Antependium   A decorative hanging, usually matching the **liturgical color**, that may cover the front of the **ambo** or **altar**; also called a **frontal**.

Antiphon   A short refrain, frequently a verse of a **psalm**, used as a repeated **congregational** response to a psalm. At **Mass**, there is a suggested **entrance antiphon** and a **communion antiphon**; the response of the **responsorial psalm** is also an antiphon. In the **Liturgy of the Hours**, antiphons are sung or recited at the beginning and end of psalms and **canticles**.

Antiphonal   A way of praying the psalms in which two **choirs** (groups) alternately **chant** or recite the verses. Originally, the term referred to the singing of a brief **antiphon** by choirs while the verses were sung by one or more soloists. Antiphonal seating is an arrangement in which the seats of the **assembly** are divided into two groups that face each other along a central aisle.

Apocalyptic   From a Greek word meaning "unveiling" or "revelation." In Christian usage it refers to the Book of Revelation (previously called the Apocalypse), the final book of the **Bible**, and images or writings based on its visions of the end of the world and the fulfillment of all creation in a new heaven and a new earth (Revelation 21:1).

Apostles' Creed   The ancient baptismal statement of the Church's faith. The questions used in the celebration of **Baptism** correspond to the statements of the Apostles' Creed. It may be used as the Profession of Faith at **Mass** and is particularly appropriate during **Lent** and **Easter Time**.

Apostolic Tradition of Hippolytus of Rome   A text which supposedly gives information on the liturgical and **ecclesial** life of the **Church** of Rome in the third century, attributed to **Hippolytus**, a Roman **presbyter**. The document now identified by this title was discovered in the nineteenth century and identified as a missing text titled the Apostolic Tradition. Although the dating and authorship of the text have more recently been questioned by scholars, the document is important for many reasons. The **Eucharistic Prayer** found in this document is the basis for the current Eucharistic Prayer II, and the prayer for the **ordination** of a **bishop** used today is also taken from this source.

Apse   The vaulted, semicircular or polygonal end of the **church** building where, in traditional Western church **architecture**, the **altar** is located.

Archangels   One of the nine **choirs** of **angels**, and specifically messengers of God. The Feast of Sts. Michael, Gabriel, and Raphael, Archangels, is celebrated on September 29.

Architecture, Liturgical   The form of architecture by which building designs meet the demands of the liturgical celebrations of the Church. New liturgical constructions must be designed in harmony with **Church** laws and must facilitate the full, conscious, and **active** **participation** of all in the liturgical action according to the various roles that make up the body of **Christ** at **worship**. General principles along with specific requirements are described in chapter 5 of the ***General Instruction of the Roman Missal*** and, for the United States, in ***Built of Living Stones: Art, Architecture, and Worship***.

Ars Celebrandi Latin for "the art of celebration." The term refers to the celebration of **liturgy** that facilitates the full, conscious, and **active participation** of the faithful, adheres to the liturgical norms, respects the various genres of liturgical language in the liturgy, makes appropriate and respectful use of the liturgical space and objects, and gives due regard to the meaning and interrelationship of the various parts of the liturgy. Discussed in Pope Benedict XVI's apostolic exhortation *Sacramentum Caritatis* (2007).

Art, Liturgical Any art form that serves the **liturgy**. Art that is appropriate for **worship** should be of good quality, express the divine presence, be appropriate for liturgical action, be able to bear the weight of **mystery**, and be made of genuine materials. Discussed in chapter 5 of the *General Instruction of the Roman Missal* and, for the United States, in *Built of Living Stones: Art, Architecture, and Worship*.

Ash Wednesday The first day of **Lent** in the **Roman Rite**, celebrated during the seventh week before **Easter**, on which **ashes** are blessed and distributed.

Ashes A **sign** of repentance on **Ash Wednesday**, made by burning **palms** or other branches blessed on the previous **Palm Sunday**. Individuals are signed with ashes on the forehead, usually in the form of a **cross**, although the ashes may also be sprinkled on the top of a person's head. One of two formulas may be used as the **minister** imposes ashes: "Repent, and believe in the **Gospel**" or "Remember that you are dust, and to dust you shall return."

Asperges The **rite** of sprinkling **holy water** on the **assembly** at **Mass**. In the current *Roman Missal*, where it is called the Rite for the **Blessing** and Sprinkling of Water, it may take the place of the **penitential act**, especially on the **Sundays** of **Easter Time**, as a reminder of **Baptism**. The sprinkling of the assembly may be accompanied by Psalm 51, with the **Latin antiphon** that begins "Asperges me" ("Sprinkle me"), or by other antiphons or **hymns**. In the **Tridentine rite**, this sprinkling may take place before the formal start of a high Mass.

Aspergil (Aspergillum)   The liturgical object used to sprinkle holy water.

Aspersorium   The small bucket or vessel that holds **holy water** and that can be carried for the purpose of sprinkling the **assembly**. Sometimes the sprinkler (**aspergil**) is called the aspersorium as well.

Assembly   The people gathered for divine **worship**, often called the **congregation**. The *Constitution on the Sacred Liturgy* (no.7), discussing the many ways **Christ** is present in the **sacrifice** of the **Mass**, says, "He is present . . . when the **Church** prays and sings, for he promised: 'Where two or three are gathered together in my name, there am I in the midst of them' (Matthew 18:20)." Contemporary liturgical theology emphasizes that it is the assembly as a whole that **celebrates** the **liturgy** under the leadership of a **priest**.

B

Baldachin (Baldacchino)   Common name for the dome-like structure built over the major **altar** in a large **church**, often supported by four or more pillars. Technically, however, the term is used only for a cloth **canopy** supported on poles that is carried over the **Blessed Sacrament** in **processions**. The term **ciborium** should be used for the dome-like structure over the altar, in addition to its more common use for a vessel for holding the Eucharistic **bread**.

Balsam   An aromatic resin derived from various plants. It is added to olive oil before it is **consecrated** as **chrism**, giving it a distinctive fragrance.

Baptism   The first and foundational Christian **sacrament**, a prerequisite for receiving all the other sacraments. By Baptism an individual is incorporated into the **Church**, the Body of **Christ**, and participates in the **priesthood of the faithful**. The **sacrament** is bestowed by **immersion** in **water** or by the pouring of water over the head. In the **Roman Rite**, this immersion or pouring is accompanied by the words, "N., I baptize you in the name of the Father, and of the Son, and of the Holy Spirit."

Baptism of the Lord   The commemoration of the **baptism** of Jesus by John in the Jordan River. It is usually celebrated on the **Sunday** after the **Epiphany**, and is considered the last day of **Christmas Time**. If the Epiphany is celebrated on January 7 or 8, the Baptism is celebrated on the Monday after the Epiphany.

Baptismal Font   The pool or basin where the **Sacrament** of **Baptism** is administered. The font may be located within the main body of the **church**, either at the entrance, or within the **nave** in the midst of the **assembly**, or in the **sanctuary**, or it may be placed in a separate **baptistery**.

Baptismal Priesthood   See **priesthood of the faithful**.

Baptismal Symbol of the Roman Church   Another term for the **Apostles' Creed**.

Baptistery   A separate section of the **church** building or even a separate building where the **baptismal font** is located and where **Baptisms** are performed; also spelled *baptistry*.

Basilica   A title of honor given by the pope to certain **churches**. A basilica outside of Rome usually enshrines two special papal insignia that are **signs** of its status: the *tintinnabulum*, a **bell** of the kind once carried in papal **processions**, and the **gold** and **red** papal *ombrellino* (umbrella). As a style of **architecture**, the ancient Roman basilica was a rectangular public building with a wide **nave**, an **apse** at one end, and colonnaded side aisles.

Beauduin, Lambert (1873–1960)   Belgian Benedictine monk and founder of the monastery of Chevetogne. He was also founding editor of the journal *Questions Liturgiques* and one of the founders of the Centre de Pastorale Liturgique in Paris. His address in 1909 at the National Congress of Catholic Works in Malines, Belgium, is seen by many as the birth of the modern **liturgical movement**.

Bell   Bells have been associated with **churches** for centuries. Large church bells housed in a steeple frequently serve as a call to **worship**, especially at 6 AM, noon, and 6 PM, for the recitation of the Angelus prayer. A bell is sometimes tolled at **funerals**. In the course of **Mass**, a small hand bell may be rung during the **Eucharistic Prayer** during the showing of each of the Eucharistic **elements** after the words of consecration. Church bells are rung during the **Gloria**

of the **Mass of the Lord's Supper** on **Holy Thursday** evening and then remain silent until the Gloria of the **Easter Vigil**.

Benedict of Nursia (c. 480–c. 547)   Founder of the **Order** of St. Benedict and considered the father of Western monasticism. The *Rule of St. Benedict* states: "Indeed, nothing is to be preferred to the Work of God" (43:3), referring to the **Liturgy of the Hours**. He encouraged the practice of *lectio divina*, a prayerful reflection and meditation on the **Word of God**.

Benediction   From **Latin** "to bless." Generally, any **blessing** is a benediction, but the term is also used for the **rite** that includes a solemn blessing with the **Blessed Sacrament** at the end of a period of **exposition** and **adoration**. The rite also includes Scripture readings, **hymns**, and **silence**.

Benedictus   The Canticle of Zechariah.

Berakah   A Hebrew prayer form that blesses God, usually beginning with "Blessed are you, **Lord** our God, King of the universe." This is the basic style of the Hebrew grace after meals, the *birkat ha-mazon*, which seems to be the ancestor of the Christian **Eucharistic Prayer**.

Bible   The fundamental book of religious writings of the Judeo-Christian tradition. The **psalms** from the Hebrew section of the Bible were the original **hymnal** for both Jewish and Christian **worship**. Sung and **proclaimed** sections from the Bible form a major part of every worship **service**.

Bidding Prayers   A term used particularly in Great Britain to refer to the intentions, or **petitions**, of the **Universal Prayer**, or **Prayer of the Faithful**. The ancient pattern of this prayer (an invitation to the **assembly** to pray, followed by **silence**, then a **collect**) was once common, but is now used only on **Good Friday**.

Birkat Ha-Mazon   From Hebrew, meaning "**blessing** of nourishment"; a Hebrew *berakah* prayed after a meal. This prayer has a threefold structure: a blessing of God, a **thanksgiving**, and an **intercession**. For some feasts, the prayer could be expanded to include a commemoration of the event being celebrated. Most scholars consider the *birkat ha-mazon* to be the immediate ancestor of the **Eucharistic Prayer**.

Bishop   The word most commonly used to translate the Greek biblical term *episkopos*, meaning "overseer" or "supervisor." The bishop heads a local community of Christians in the territorial area called a diocese. Bishop is the final of the three **orders** of ministry that may be received through the **Sacrament** of **Holy Orders**: **deacon**, **priest**, and bishop.

Bishops' Committee on Divine Worship   The department of the **United States Conference of Catholic Bishops** that assists the **bishops** in matters related to the **liturgy**. It is a standing committee made up of bishops, assisted by a group of consultants who are experts in liturgical theology, with an office (secretariat) that carries out the work of the committee.

Blessed Sacrament   The name commonly used to refer to the Eucharistic **elements** of **bread** and **wine** after they have been **consecrated** and have become the Body and Blood of **Christ**.

Blessed Sacrament Chapel   A separate **chapel** in which the **tabernacle** with the reserved **Blessed Sacrament** is located.

Blessing   Any prayer that praises and thanks God. In particular, *blessing* describes those prayers in which God is praised because of some person or object, and thus the individual or object is seen to have become specially dedicated or sanctified because of the prayer of faith. Many blessing prayers ask God's favor toward a person in time of need or on a special occasion. Liturgical celebrations usually conclude with a blessing pronounced over the **assembly**.

Boat   See incense boat.

Book of Blessings   The **ritual** book that contains **blessings** for numerous occasions. Many of the blessings may be given during the celebration of **Mass**, and so most of the **rites** include forms both for within Mass and outside Mass. In a number of cases, the **rubrics** specify that a **lay minister** may lead a particular ritual outside Mass.

Book of Common Prayer   The main **service** book of the **Church** of England and other member churches of the Anglican Communion. Some other Protestant churches also use this title for their service books. It includes texts for the celebration of the **Eucharist**, various **sacraments**, funerals and other **services**, and the **Divine Office**.

Book of the Elect   A book into which the names of those **catechumens** who have been chosen, or elected, for initiation at the next **Easter Vigil**, are written at or before the **Rite of Election**.

Book of the Gospels   A **ritual** book from which the passages from the **Gospels** prescribed for **Masses** on **Sundays**, **solemnities**, **feasts** of the **Lord** and of the **saints**, and ritual Masses are proclaimed; also called an **evangeliary**. It may be carried in the **entrance procession** and placed on the **altar**, and then processed to the **ambo** during the **Gospel Acclamation**. It is presented to **deacons** at their **ordination** and held over the heads of **bishops** at their ordination.

Botte, Bernard (1893–1980)   Belgian Benedictine liturgist. He is known for his historical studies and critical editions of numerous ancient liturgical texts. He was highly influential in the liturgical renewal centers of Paris and was a key figure in the revision of the **rites** of **ordination**. He also participated in the 1960s revision of the **Mass** as a consultor to the **Consilium**.

Bouyer, Louis (1913–2004)   Member of the French Congregation of the Oratory and prominent in the liturgical movement. He authored many books, including *Rite and Man: Natural Sacredness and Christian Liturgy*; *Liturgical Piety*; and *Eucharist: Theology and Spirituality of the Eucharistic Prayer*.

Bow   An inclination of either the upper half of the body (that is, a bow at the waist, called a **profound bow**) or of the head (called a simple bow) as a **sign** of respect for certain individuals and sacred objects. Paragraph 275 of the ***General Instruction of the Roman Missal*** describes the different bows that are appropriate during the celebration of the **Eucharist**.

Brazier   A bowl-type vessel used for the burning of **incense**.

Bread   Bread and **wine**, through the celebration of the **Eucharist**, become the Body and Blood of the **Lord** Jesus **Christ**. They are the essential **elements**, the **matter**, for this **sacrament**. Bread for the Eucharist must be made solely from wheat flour and **water**; in the **Roman Rite** it must be unleavened. It should appear as food and, ideally, one large loaf should be used, which can be broken into many pieces.

Breaking of the Bread   The name by which the Eucharistic **liturgy** was called in the ancient Church, according to the Acts of the Apostles (2:42). The action of breaking the **bread** is based on the biblical references to the action of Jesus at the **Last Supper** (Matthew 26:26, Luke 24:30, 35). It is also the term formerly used for the **fraction of the Bread** at **Mass**.

Breviary   The name commonly given to the book containing the **Liturgy of the Hours**. The word is derived from the **Latin** word for "abridgement" or "summary" because the format used by most **priests** was abridged from the monastic format, which often uses several books for a single **office**.

Built of Living Stones: Art, Architecture, and Worship
A document from the **United States Conference of Catholic Bishops,** approved in 2000, that gives guidelines, norms, theological perspectives, and practical information for **art, architecture,** and furnishings in the building and renovating of **churches** in the United States. The document builds on and replaces its predecessor, *Environment and Art in Catholic Worship* (1978).

Burse (1) A small, purse-like container, frequently attached to a string, into which a **pyx** for bringing **Holy Communion** to the sick can be placed.
   (2) The flat, square, fabric-covered case into which a folded **corporal** may be placed. It is not used in the current Roman **Rite.**

Byzantine Catholic Churches Some of the twenty-three autonomous Eastern **Churches** in communion with the Bishop of Rome, which, with the Roman Catholic Church, make up the Catholic Church. They follow the **Byzantine Rite** in their liturgies and, like all the Eastern Catholic Churches, maintain their own laws and customs. Melkite Catholics, Ukrainian Catholics, Ruthenian Catholics, and Romanian Catholics are some of the Byzantine Catholic Churches common in the United States.

Byzantine Rite The **ritual** system that developed from the city of Byzantium—renamed Constantinople, and now called Istanbul—in present-day Turkey. It is used in the **Byzantine Catholic Churches** and by Orthodox Christians. Byzantine Rite churches are distinguished by an **iconastasis,** and the **liturgy** is **celebrated** with much singing, **incense,** and elaborate ritual.

C

Candidate   In its broadest definition, the term refers to anyone preparing to receive a **sacrament**. In the *Rite of Christian Initiation of Adults*, the term is used as a general designation for **adults** who are expressing an interest in the Catholic faith, whether baptized or not. In common usage, *candidate* is used for a baptized person preparing for reception into the full communion of the Catholic **Church**; an unbaptized person inquiring about preparing for Christian initiation is called an **inquirer**.

Candle   A lamp that has a living flame. For the celebration of **Mass**, two, four, or six candles may be used, and seven may be used when the **diocesan bishop** celebrates Mass. Candles used for Mass must be made of wax.

Candlemas   Another name for the **Feast of the Presentation of the Lord**, celebrated on February 2. The name derives from the **blessing** of **candles** and **procession** that may take place at **Mass** on that day.

Canon   (1) An older name for the **Eucharistic Prayer**, especially the section after the **Holy, Holy, Holy**. The title **Roman Canon**, which is now used as the subtitle of Eucharistic Prayer I in *The Roman Missal*, reflects the older usage.
   (2) *Canon* may also refer to a law or rule. The *Code of Canon Law*, revised in 1983, is the official collection of ecclesiastical laws governing the Roman Catholic **Church**. The *Code of Canons of the Eastern Churches*, published in 1990, governs the Eastern Catholic Churches.

(3) A *canon* may also be one of a group of **priests** who live in community according to a rule.

(4) *Canon* may also refer to an authoritative list, particularly the list of books that make up the **Bible**.

Canonical Hours   The liturgies of prayer and praise that form the **Liturgy of the Hours** and are celebrated at certain prescribed times of the day. The hours are **Morning Prayer**, **Midmorning Prayer**, **Midday Prayer**, **Midafternoon Prayer**, **Evening Prayer**, **Night Prayer**, and the **Office of Readings**.

Canopy   A cloth supported by four poles under which the **Blessed Sacrament** is carried in **procession**. It also refers to the **baldacchino** of the **altar**.

Canticle   A **hymn**, particularly one taken from **Sacred Scripture**, though *not* from the **psalms**. During **Morning Prayer**, the second selection during the **psalmody** is a canticle taken from the Old Testament, and during **Evening Prayer**, the third selection during the psalmody is a canticle taken from one of the New Testament letters. The **Gospel canticles**—the **Canticle of Zechariah**, the **Canticle of Mary**, and the **Canticle of Simeon**—are a feature of the offices of Morning, Evening, and **Night Prayer**.

Canticle of Mary   Mary's song of praise, found at Luke 1:46–55, by which she responds to the greeting of Elizabeth that she is blessed among women. It is also called the **Magnificat**, from the beginning of the **canticle** in **Latin**, "Magnificat anima mea Dominum" ("My soul **proclaims** the greatness of the **Lord**"). It is sung or said during **Evening Prayer**.

Canticle of Simeon   Simeon's words upon seeing the child Jesus at his presentation in the Temple of Jerusalem, found at Luke 2:29–32. It is also called the **Nunc Dimittis**, from the first words of the **canticle** in **Latin**, meaning "Lord, now you let your servant go in peace." It is sung or said during **Night Prayer**.

Canticle of Zechariah   The prophecy of Zechariah, found at Luke 1:68–79, which he **proclaimed** at the circumcision of his son, who would be known as John the Baptist. It is also called the **Benedictus** from the first words of the **canticle** in **Latin**, "Benedictus Dominus Deus Israel" ("Blessed be the **Lord**, the God of Israel"). It is sung or said during **Morning Prayer**.

Cantor   A liturgical **minister** who leads the singing of the **assembly** at a **liturgy**. The cantor may also sing alone, such as singing the verses of the **responsorial psalm**.

Casel, Odo (1886–1948)   Monk of the Benedictine monastery of **Maria Laach** in Germany. He developed the "**mystery**-theology" as an attempt to explain how the divine is present in Christian **worship**, one of the first modern attempts to develop a contemporary liturgical theology. *The Mystery of Christian Worship* is perhaps Casel's most famous work. He suffered a stroke as he began to intone the **Exsultet** at the **Easter Vigil** in 1948 and died a few hours later.

Cassock   A long-sleeved, ankle-length garment worn by seminarians, **priests**, and **bishops**. The cassock is usually black, although priests with the title of monsignor wear either a cassock with purple trim or a purple cassock, depending on their rank, and bishops wear a purple cassock; the pope wears a white cassock, as do other clergy in tropical climates. In some parishes, **altar servers** wear a black or red cassock with a **surplice**.

Catechetical Age   Usually considered to be seven years of age; also called the **age of reason** or the age of discretion. For the purpose of Christian initiation, a person who has reached catechetical age is considered an **adult** and is to be initiated into the **Church** according to the *Rite of Christian Initiation of Adults* and catechized according to their needs. A person baptized after having reached the age of reason is to receive all three **sacraments of initiation**. Before this age, the person is considered an infant and is baptized using the *Rite of Baptism for Children*.

Catechumen   An unbaptized person who has declared their intention to prepare for the **sacraments of initiation** and has been accepted into the **order** of catechumens. Catechumens, though not yet fully initiated, are joined to the **Church** and are considered part of the household of **Christ**. The names of those accepted as catechumens are to be written in the **register of catechumens** kept by the parish.

Catechumenate   The second of four periods in the process of Christian initiation as described in the *Rite of Christian Initiation of Adults*. The period begins with the Rite of Acceptance into the **order of catechumens**. It should last long enough for the nurturing and growth of the catechumens' faith and conversion to God; in the United States, it is expected to last at least a year, but it may vary according to progress and prior formation of the individual. Sometimes the term *catechumenate* is used to refer to the entire initiation process.

Cathedra   The **bishop's** chair in a cathedral **church**. The cathedra is a **sign** of the bishop's leadership and teaching authority. The bishop alone uses it as the **presidential chair** at **liturgy** in cathedral.

Cathedral   The principal **church** in a diocese; the term derives from the **cathedra**. The cathedral is the usual site for the celebration of major diocesan liturgies, such as the **Chrism Mass**, **ordinations**, and Rites of Election.

Celebrant   The **presiding minister** at **worship**. Hence, the presiding **priest** at **Mass** may be referred to as the celebrant. Use of the term in this sense must be balanced, however, by the emphasis in contemporary liturgical theology that all those in the liturgical **assembly**—**priest** and people alike—**celebrate** the **Mass** and together offer the **sacrifice** to God.

Celebrate   To enact a **worship service**—for example, "We celebrate Mass." The word is used both of the action of the **priest** or bishop, who may be said to "celebrate the Mass," and to the action of the entire **assembly**. While the common meaning of the term suggests a festive gathering, all liturgies, whether solemn or joyful, are called celebrations.

Celebration of the Passion of the Lord   The primary **liturgy** celebrated on **Good Friday**. It consists of the **Liturgy of the Word**, with the proclamation of the Passion according to St. John; **solemn intercessions**; adoration of the Holy **Cross**; and **Holy Communion**.

Censer   Another name for a **thurible**.

Censer Bearer   Another name for a **thurifer**.

Ceremonial of Bishops   The official book of directions and **rubrics** to aid **bishops** in celebrating the **Mass**, the **sacraments**, and other liturgies. The rubrics of the *Ceremonial of Bishops* are much more detailed than those in ***The Roman Missal***, and thus the *Ceremonial of Bishops* is frequently an aid to understanding the rubrics in the Missal. The current edition was issued in 1984.

Chalice   The sacred vessel, usually a stemmed cup, used to hold the **wine** that is **consecrated** during the **Mass**.

Chalice Veil   A square cloth that may be draped over the **chalice** before it is brought to the **altar** for the **Liturgy of the Eucharist**. Its use is optional.

Chancel   Another name for the **sanctuary**, although in some **churches** the chancel may include the **choir** area in addition to the sanctuary.

Chant   A sung text that is an integral part of the **liturgy**, such as the **entrance chant** and the **communion chant**. The term also refers to the actual singing of such texts.

Chapel   A small building or a defined space within a larger **church** or other building designated for private prayer or liturgical **worship**. A **reservation chapel** would include the **tabernacle** containing the **Blessed Sacrament**.

Chasuble   The outer **vestment** of **priests** and **bishops** worn while celebrating the **Eucharist**. It is a large, sleeveless garment with a simple opening for the head worn over the **stole** and **alb**. The color of the chasuble matches the **liturgical color** of the **feast** or liturgical **time**.

Child   For the purposes of Christian initiation, one who has not yet reached the age of discernment (age of reason, presumed to be seven years of age) and therefore cannot profess personal faith. Children younger than seven are baptized using the *Rite of Baptism for Children*. The initiation of children older than seven should follow the pattern of the *Rite of Christian Initiation of Adults*, with the adaptations given for children of **catechetical age**.

Choir   A select group of singers who sing during the liturgical **rites** of the **Church**. The choir supports the singing of the entire **assembly** and should not dominate or replace the **congregational** singing. Like all liturgical **ministers**, the choir is to facilitate the full, conscious, and **active participation** of all. *Choir* can also refer to a separate **chapel** where seats (choir stalls) are arranged so that one half of the assembly faces the other half, especially where the assembly prays the **Liturgy of the Hours** "in choir."

Choir Dress   The liturgical attire of **bishops** and **priests** worn when they are present at but not celebrating or concelebrating **Mass**, and at non-Eucharistic liturgies; essentially a **cassock** with a **rochet** or a **surplice**. Further norms are described in the *Ceremonial of Bishops*.

Chrism One of the three **holy oils**. It is **consecrated** by the **bishop** at the **Chrism Mass** and used at the **Baptism** of infants, at **Confirmation**, at the **ordination** of **priests** and bishops, and at the dedication of **churches** and **altars**. Chrism is scented, usually with **balsam**, which creates a distinctive and pleasing aroma; it is the only one of the three sacramental oils that is scented. Chrism is stored in the **ambry** and in **oil stocks** that are often labeled SC, for "sacred chrism."

Chrism Mass The **Mass** celebrated on the morning of **Holy Thursday** (or another day close to **Easter**) at which the **bishop** **blesses** the **oil of catechumens** and **oil of the sick** and **consecrates** the **chrism** that will be used in the celebration of the **sacraments** throughout the coming year. The celebration of the Chrism Mass also includes the renewal by the **priests** and the bishop(s) of their commitment to priestly ministry.

Chrismation The name used in the Eastern Churches for the sacrament known in the Roman Rite as Confirmation.

Christ A term derived from the Greek meaning "anointed," used as a title for Jesus of Nazareth. It is the equivalent of *Messiah*, *anointed* in Hebrew, which is used in the Old Testament to designate the Promised One to be sent by God to be the king and savior of Israel.

Christe, Eleison Greek for "**Christ**, have mercy." It is an **invocation** used in **litanies**, particularly in the **penitential act** where it is sung alternately with **Kyrie eleison** ("**Lord**, have mercy").

Christian Witness A baptized non-Catholic who acts as a witness at **Baptism**. The non-Catholic must be a validly baptized, believing Christian and can act in this capacity only along with a Catholic godparent.

Christmas Time   The period of the **liturgical year** beginning with **Evening Prayer** I of the **Nativity of the Lord** and ending with Evening Prayer on the **Feast** of the **Baptism of the Lord** (which may fall on the **Sunday** or Monday after **Epiphany**). This liturgical **time** commemorates the Incarnation, the birth of **Christ**, and his first manifestations.

Church   The community of Christians. The building for **worship** was originally called the "house of the Church" but now the word *church* also refers to the building itself. The word is also used to refer to those involved in the administration of the community of Christians, particularly the **hierarchy**, the "institutional church."

Ciborium   The liturgical vessel used for the Eucharistic **bread**. Although many ciboria resemble **chalices**, contemporary ciboria are more commonly made in the form of bowls. Both styles frequently are made with a covering lid. The **canopy** or **baldacchino** over an **altar** is sometimes called a ciborium.

Cincture   The cord used to secure an **alb** at the waist. It is usually white, although it may also match the **color** of the liturgical **time**. Its use is optional.

Circular Letter Concerning the Preparation and Celebration of the Easter Feasts   A document issued by the **Congregation for Divine Worship** in 1988, also known by its **Latin** title *Paschale Solemnitatis*, which contains norms, regulations, and various other pastoral and doctrinal elements concerning **Lent**, **Holy Week**, the **Sacred Paschal Triduum**, and **Easter Time**.

Closing Prayer   A term that is sometimes used to refer to what is properly called the **prayer after communion**. The term may be applied to a prayer that concludes other liturgies, although *concluding prayer* is more frequently used in the **ritual** books.

Collect   The **opening prayer** of the **Mass**. It sums up or collects the thoughts and prayers of the **assembly**, and concludes the **Introductory Rites**. After the collect, everyone is seated and the **Liturgy of the Word** begins. By tradition, the same prayer used as the collect of the Mass is also used as the concluding prayer for **Morning Prayer** and **Evening Prayer**.

Collection   The action of collecting money for the **Church** and the poor that takes place at **Mass** after the **Universal Prayer**. These **offerings** of money may be brought forward along with the **bread** and **wine** in the **procession**, because they are a **sign** of the self-offering of the members of the **assembly** participating in the offering of the **sacrifice**.

Colors, Liturgical   The official colors of the outer **vestments** worn by **celebrants** and assisting **deacons**. Each day in the **liturgical calendar** requires a specific color or offers a choice among colors depending upon the liturgical **time** or the particular **Mass** being celebrated. By tradition in the **Roman Rite**, the colors are **white**, **green**, **red**, **violet**, black, and **rose**; the determination of which color is used is found in *The Roman Missal* and in the *General Instruction of the Roman Missal*. More precious vestments, usually with **gold** or **silver** threads, may be worn on solemn occasions.

Commemoration   A liturgical designation given to **memorials** that fall on the weekdays of **Lent** and from December 17 to 31. Because the weekdays of Lent, the weekdays of **Advent** from December 17 to 24, and the days within the **Octave** of Christmas have a higher liturgical rank than memorials, and therefore take precedence over them, all memorials, both obligatory and optional, are considered optional and may be celebrated only as commemorations. This means that at **Mass** the prayer of the **saint** may replace the **collect** of the weekday, but all other texts are taken from those of the seasonal weekday.

Commemoration of All the Faithful Departed   Liturgical title for November 2, commonly called **All Souls' Day**, the day the **Church** remembers and prays for all her deceased members. The day has a unique status in that it does not have a designation as a **solemnity**, **feast**, or **memorial**, and yet it replaces the **Mass** for the **Sunday** in **Ordinary Time** when it falls on a Sunday.

Commendation of the Dying   The prayers for a dying person, found in *Pastoral Care of the Sick: Rites of Anointing and Viaticum*. The prayers are meant to assist the dying to face death with faith and trust by being united to Jesus' own Death, and to bring consolation to those who are present. They include Scripture passages, the **Litany of the Saints**, and the Prayer of Commendation. The **rites** may be led by a **priest**, **deacon**, or layperson.

Commentator   A **minister** who provides explanations of sacred texts or actions to the **assembly** during **Mass**, as described in the *General Instruction of the Roman Missal*. The function of commentator was widely used in the years immediately following the earliest liturgical reforms following the Second Vatican Council. It is infrequently used today.

Commingling   The **rite** of dropping a small particle of the **consecrated bread** into the **chalice**. It occurs in the **Mass** after the fraction and seems to have its origin in the rite of dropping a piece of bread (called the *fermentum*) consecrated by the pope and brought to the celebrations in outlying areas of Rome.

Commissioning   A term used for the authorizing and **blessing** of individuals to function as **extraordinary ministers of Holy Communion**. It may also be used in a general sense for the blessing or authorization of laypersons to function in any liturgical **ministry**.

Committee on Divine Worship   See Bishop's Committee on Divine Worship.

Common   Term used for groups of texts in *The Roman Missal* and the **Liturgy of the Hours** that are used on **feasts** and **memorials** that do not have their own particular, or **proper**, texts assigned to them. Examples are the Common of the Blessed Virgin Mary, the Common of **Martyrs**, the Common of Pastors, and the Common of Holy Men and Women.

Communal Penance Service   Common and popular title used for the **Rite** for **Reconciliation** of Several **Penitents** with Individual Confession and Absolution as found in the *Rite of Penance*. Such a **service** would include a **Liturgy of the Word**, a communal **examination of conscience**, and individual **confession** and **absolution**. The title "Communal Penance Service" may also broadly, though somewhat incorrectly, be used to refer to what are more properly called **penitential services**, that is, gatherings of the **People of God** to hear God's Word but without individual confessions and sacramental absolution. Such penitential services are also described in the **ritual** book *Rite of Penance*.

Communicant   A person who receives **Holy Communion**.

Communicantes   Name given to that paragraph in **Eucharistic Prayer** I that begins, "In communion with those whose memory we venerate." It expresses the **assembly**'s union with the **saints** in the **offering** of the **sacrifice**. There are special forms of the Communicantes for the **Nativity of the Lord** and its **octave**, on the **Epiphany** of the Lord, at the **Mass of the Lord's Supper**, from the **Easter Vigil** until the Second Sunday of **Easter**, on the **Ascension of the Lord**, and on **Pentecost Sunday**.

Communion Antiphon   A verse from **Sacred Scripture** provided in *The Roman Missal* that may be sung or said during the reception of **Holy Communion** at **Mass**. Originally, the antiphon was the refrain from a **psalm** that was **chanted** during Holy Communion, which is still an option in the current Roman Missal.

Communion Rail   The railing found at the edge of the **sanctuary** in many **churches** at which **communicants** would kneel while receiving **Holy Communion**.

Communion Rite   The portion of the **Mass** that begins immediately after the **Amen** of the **Eucharistic Prayer** and ends with the **prayer after communion**. It includes the **Lord's Prayer**, the **sign of peace**, the **fraction of the Bread**, and the reception of **Holy Communion**.

***Competentes* ("Copetitioners")**   A title that can be applied to the **elect**, that is, those **adults** who are in the final stage of preparation for the reception of the **sacraments of initiation**. It refers to the fact that they are joined together in asking for and aspiring to receive the sacraments.

Compline   An older name for **Night Prayer** from the **Latin** term for this **office**.

Concelebrant   A **priest** or **bishop** who **celebrates Mass** with other priests or bishops according to the norms for **concelebration**.

Concelebration   The form of **Mass** in which several **priests** **celebrate** according to the norms for concelebration. One priest fulfills the role of **priest celebrant**, but all the concelebrating priests are considered to be offering the Mass. Except for Masses of **Ordination**, concelebration was forbidden in the **Roman Rite** before the Second Vatican Council, though it was common in almost all Eastern Rites. The **rubrics** for concelebration are found in the *General Instruction of the Roman Missal*.

Concluding Rites   The last part of the **Mass**, following the **Communion Rite**. It consists of brief announcements, a **greeting**, a **blessing**, and the **dismissal** of the **assembly**. If an additional **rite** follows the Mass, such as the **Final Commendation** at a funeral or a **procession** with the **Blessed Sacrament**, that rite replaces the Concluding Rites of the Mass. The term can also refer to the closing rites in any **liturgy**.

Concomitance   The doctrine that teaches that **Christ** is fully present under each of the **Eucharistic species**. Thus, a **communicant** who receives **Holy Communion** under the form of **bread** alone or **wine** alone receives both the Body and the Blood of Christ, not only the Body of Christ or the Blood of Christ. This does not negate the importance of the fuller **sign** value of receiving **Holy Communion under both kinds**.

Confession   The common term used for the **Sacrament** of **Penance** and Reconciliation. The term also refers to the actual oral naming of sins that takes place as one part of the celebration of that sacrament.

Confessional   The place where the **Sacrament of Penance** is **celebrated**. In a traditional confessional, the **priest** sits in a central booth while the **penitent**, located in an adjoining booth, kneels facing the **confessor** and speaking to him through an opaque grate. A larger place for the sacrament, often referred to as a **reconciliation chapel**, may allow the penitent the choice to sit and speak to the priest face to face or to remain behind a screen or curtain, in accord with norms for the United States decreed by the National Conference of Catholic Bishops in 1999.

Confessor   (1) A **priest** who is qualified to hear **confession** and to grant sacramental **absolution**. The term is often used to designate a particular priest to whom one confesses on a regular basis ("Father N. is my confessor").

(2) In the ancient **Church**, a Christian who suffered punishment for professing faith in **Christ**, but was not killed. The person thus confessed the faith under persecution.

Confirmation   The **sacrament** that continues the initiation process begun in **Baptism** and marks the sealing of the Holy Spirit. It is administered through an **anointing** with **chrism** on the forehead with the words, "N., be sealed with the Gift of the Holy Spirit," preceded by the **imposition of hands**. **Adults** who are initiated into the **Church** receive Baptism, Confirmation, and **Eucharist** at one celebration. In the United States, those baptized as infants commonly receive Confirmation years after receiving **Holy Communion** for the first time, although some bishops have begun celebrating Confirmation before First Communion, or at the same **liturgy**.

Confiteor   A common name given to the **confession** of sinfulness used in one form of the **penitential act** at **Mass**. The name is derived from the first word of the **Latin** version, "Confiteor Deo omnipotenti" ("I confess to almighty God").

Congregation   The community of Christians gathered for **worship**, also called the **assembly**. Sometimes the term is used to refer to the "people in the **pews**" to distinguish them from the clergy, the **choir**, and other liturgical **ministers**.

Congregation for Divine Worship and the Discipline of the Sacraments   One of the departments of the Roman Curia. It has responsibility for all matters relating to the **liturgy** and **sacraments** in the **Church**, performing duties in the name of the pope and with his authority.

Consecrate   To make holy and set apart through prayer. The term is specifically used at **Mass** in reference to the **bread** and **wine**, which by **consecration** become the Body and Blood of **Christ**; at the **Chrism Mass** in reference to the sacred chrism; and in the *Roman Pontifical,* in the **rite** titled "Consecration to a Life of Virginity." In the past, the **ordination** of a **bishop** was referred to as a consecration, but the term is not used in the current Rite of Ordination. It is still retained, however, in **canon** 379 of the 1983 *Code of Canon Law.*

Consecration   That portion of the **Institution Narrative** in the **Eucharistic Prayer** when the **priest** pronounces the words of **Christ** at the **Last Supper** and the **bread** and **wine** are transformed into the Body and Blood of Christ. While Roman Catholics point to Christ's words as the moment of consecration, the entire Eucharistic Prayer is consecratory.

Consent   The liturgical and canonical term for the **marriage** vows; the bride and groom are said to declare or exchange their consent. The term goes back to ancient Rome, and implies the internal covenant of love and life and the external expression of that covenant through the words of the vows.

Consilium   The common title for the Consilium ad exsequendam Constitutionem de Sacra Liturgia, a special commission which was established in 1964 and absorbed into the **Congregation for Divine Worship** in 1970. It consisted of two main groups: forty (full) members (mostly cardinals and **bishops**) who had deliberative vote, and a much larger group of consultors, who were most often experts in **liturgy** or liturgical history. It was this body that revised the **Order** of **Mass** and the **rites** of the various **sacraments**. Among its consultors were **Bernard Botte**, OSB, **Godfrey Diekmann**, OSB, **Josef Jungmann**, SJ, and **Frederick McManus**.

Constitution on the Sacred Liturgy   The first document of the Second Vatican Council, promulgated on December 4, 1963, also known by its **Latin** title, *Sacrosanctum Concilium*. It allowed the celebration of liturgical rites in the **vernacular**, called for the full, conscious, and **active participation** of the **assembly**, and ordered the revision of all liturgical **rites**.

Consubstantial   From the **Latin** *consubstantialis*, meaning "of one essence or **substance**." The term appears in the **Niceno-Constantinopolitan Creed**, in the translation currently used at **Mass**; it was formerly translated as "one in being." It refers to the doctrine that Jesus **Christ** is of the same substance as the Father and is fully divine.

Contrition   The heartfelt sorrow for sin and the intention to avoid it in the future.

Conventual Mass   The major daily **Mass celebrated** by members of a religious community, usually in the **chapel** of the religious community.

Cope   A long, cape-like **vestment**. It may be worn in **processions** joined to a **Mass** (for example, the procession with **palms** on Palm **Sunday**) or at more solemn liturgical celebrations that occur outside Mass (for example, the **Liturgy of the Hours** or **Benediction**). The cope is normally worn only by an ordained **minister**.

Corporal   The cloth placed on the **altar** on which the vessels containing **bread** and **wine** are placed. It is traditionally square and is placed on top of the **altar cloth**. Its purpose is to catch any fragments of the **Blessed Sacrament** that may fall onto the altar.

Corpus Christi   **Latin** for "Body of **Christ**." It was the Latin title for the **Feast** of the Body of Christ, which was merged with the Feast of the **Precious Blood** in the 1969 reform of the calendar; it is now **celebrated** as the **Solemnity** of the Most Holy Body and Blood of Christ.

Council of Trent   The nineteenth Ecumenical Council of the **Church**, which opened December 13, 1545, and closed on December 4, 1563. It was convoked to respond to the Protestant **Reformation** and to bring about a reform of the inner life of the Church. The liturgical reforms that resulted were the reform of the **Breviary** in 1568 and the reform of the **Missal** in 1570. The term *Tridentine Mass* refers to the 1570 *Roman Missal* promulgated by Pope Pius V.

Cranmer, Thomas (1489–1556)   Archbishop of Canterbury at the time of King Henry VIII and the establishment of the independent **Church** of England. He was responsible for the change of the **Latin rites** into English and for the compilation of the first two Anglican **Books of Common Prayer** of 1549 and 1552.

Credence Table   The side table on which the vessels and articles needed for the celebration are placed when not in use, particularly during the celebration of the **Eucharist**.

Creed   Another name for the **Profession of Faith**, or **Symbol**.

Cremated Remains   The remains of the human body after it has been cremated. This term is preferred over "cremains," a funeral industry term, affording greater dignity to the deceased. By virtue of an **indult** granted by the **Congregation for Divine Worship and the Discipline of the Sacraments** in 1997, the **Funeral Liturgy** may be celebrated with the cremated remains present.

Cremation   The reduction of a dead body to ashes as a result of fire or intense heat. Cremation is permitted by the Roman Catholic **Church** as long as it is not done for a reason that is contrary to Christian teaching.

Crosier   The common name for the **pastoral staff** of a **bishop**.

Crosier Bearer   The **minister** who holds the **bishop's crosier** at liturgy when the bishop himself is not holding it. This minister may also take the crosier to and from the bishop as needed.

Cross   Any representation of the Cross on which **Christ** died. When a cross has a figure of Christ crucified, it is usually referred to as a **crucifix**.

Cross Bearer   The liturgical **minister** who carries the **processional cross** at liturgies, sometimes called a **crucifer**.

Crucifix   A cross that has the image of **Christ** crucified on it.

Crucifer   The liturgical **minister** who carries the **processional** cross at liturgies, sometimes called a **cross bearer**.

Cruet   A vessel, often a small pitcher, containing the **wine** or the **water** used in the celebration of the **Eucharist**.

Cult   A system of **worship**, with particular reference to external ceremonies. The word can refer both to **rites** comprising divine worship and also to the devotions by which external honor is given to **saints**. In the secular realm, the word is often used in a pejorative manner to indicate certain religious groups typified by secrecy and the separation of members from those outside the group.

Cyril of Alexandria (d. 444)   **Bishop** of Alexandria, **doctor** of the Western **Church**. He was a theologian at the Council of Ephesus who opposed the Nestorians and defended the title of Mary as **Theotokos**, God-bearer, a title used in the Byzantine **liturgy** to this day.

Cyril of Jerusalem (d. 387)   **Bishop** of Jerusalem, Doctor of the Western **Church**. Cyril is author of the *Mystagogical Catecheses*, a series of lectures to the newly baptized. This work offers a description of the various **rites**, particularly of the **baptismal** rites as **celebrated** in his day. His instruction on how to receive communion in the hand is often quoted: "Make your left hand a throne for the right, since it is to receive a king" (Lecture 5:21). He is quoted in support of the theology that says that it is the **epiclesis** that effects the change of **bread** and **wine** into the Body and Blood of Christ: "The bread of the Eucharist, after the **invocation** of the Holy Spirit, is mere bread no longer, but the Body of Christ" (Lecture 3:3), "for whatsoever the Holy Spirit has touched is sanctified and changed" (Lecture 5:7). He had great influence on the rites of **Holy Week**, and the elaborate and extensive rites he celebrated were documented by the pilgrim **Egeria**.

D

Daily Office   Another term for the **Divine Office** or the **Liturgy of the Hours**.

Dalmatic   The sleeved outer **vestment** proper to a **deacon**, worn over the **alb** and **stole**. The **color** of the dalmatic matches the **liturgical color** of the **feast** or liturgical **time**.

Daniélou, Jean (1905–1974)   French Jesuit **priest** and later cardinal. He rediscovered patristic exegesis, both of Scripture and of **liturgy**. He was the author of numerous works, most notably *The Bible and the Liturgy*.

Daytime Prayer   Collective name for **Midmorning Prayer**, **Midday Prayer**, and **Midafternoon Prayer** in the **Liturgy of the Hours**. Each of these prayers consists of an introductory verse, a **hymn**, **psalmody**, a short Scripture reading, a verse following the reading, a concluding prayer, and an **acclamation**. Although there are three distinct daytime hours, only those religious communities bound to praying the hours in **choir** must pray all three; others may choose to pray only one of them.

Deacon   An ordained **minister** of the Catholic **Church** belonging to the first of the three **orders** of ordained ministry that may be received through the **Sacrament** of **Holy Orders**: deacon, **priest**, and **bishop**. Deacons are ordained for the service of charity in the world as well as for liturgical ministry. Their liturgical duties at **Mass** include **proclaiming** the **Gospel**, announcing the intentions of the **Universal Prayer**, assisting the **priest** at the **altar**, administering the **Precious Blood** to the faithful, and dismissing the people at the end of Mass.

Deaconess A female **minister** in the early **Church** whose major duties were to assist in the **Baptism** and **anointing** of women. Although deaconesses were common in some parts of the East, they have generally ceased to exist. Ancient texts for the **blessing** and installation of deaconesses have been found, but it is unclear whether deaconesses were considered equivalent to male **deacons**.

Dedication of a Church The formal, solemn **blessing** of a church building for sacred use. The **ritual** book *Dedication of a Church and an Altar* gives the various **rites** for dedicating a **church** and an **altar**.

Deprecative Form The prayer form in which God is asked to perform an act of grace. For example, in the ***Order of Celebrating Matrimony***, two options for **blessing** the **rings** are in the deprecative form: "Bless, O **Lord**, these rings which we bless in your name . . . " and "Bless and **sanctify** your servants in their love, O Lord . . . " Alternative forms for such liturgical texts are called **indicative** or **invocative**.

Diaconate The term for the **order** of **deacon**, the first of the three orders of ordained ministry in the Catholic **Church**.

Didache An early Christian collection of catechetical and liturgical texts, parts of which seem to date to the mid-first century of the Christian era. Many suggest it was edited around the year 75. The title is the Greek word for *teaching*. Contained in the *Didache* are the texts for the **Lord's Prayer**, the **Rite** of **Baptism**, regulations on **fasting**, and prayers over the **bread** and **chalice** (cup). It is uncertain whether the prayers over the bread and chalice were used at a **Eucharist** in our sense, or at an **agape** meal, or whether any distinction would have been made in the **Church** at that time.

Diekmann, Godfrey (1908–2002) American Benedictine liturgist and author of *Come, Let Us Worship*, among other works. He was editor-in-chief of the journal *Worship* (originally **Orate Fratres**) until the early 1980s. He was one of the few Americans appointed as a consultor to the postconciliar commission (the **Consilium**) that revised the **Order** of **Mass** after the Second Vatican Council.

Diocesan Bishop   The **bishop** in charge of a diocese, sometimes referred to as the **ordinary**. Among many administrative and pastoral duties, the diocesan bishop oversees and directs all sacramental and liturgical celebrations in the diocese and is considered the chief liturgist of the diocese.

Diptych   In the early **Church**, a double-paneled tablet on which the names of those commemorated at the Eucharistic **liturgy** were listed. In the Eastern Churches the term is used of the list itself, or even of the **intercessions** section of the **Eucharistic Prayer** in which the living and the dead are commemorated.

Directory on Popular Piety and the Liturgy   A document issued by the **Congregation for Divine Worship and the Discipline of the Sacraments** in 2001 that discusses the proper relationship between the official **liturgy** of the **Church** and expressions of popular piety, offering both theological principles and practical guidelines.

Dismissal   The final, formal invitation by the **deacon** or, in his absence, the **priest** for the **assembly** to go forth from the liturgical celebration. The word can also refer to the dismissal of the **catechumens** after the **homily** at **Mass**.

Divine Office   Another name for the **Liturgy of the Hours**.

Divine Praises   A prayer of praise consisting of **acclamations** that bless God the Father, Jesus **Christ**, the Holy Spirit, the Blessed Virgin Mary, St. Joseph, and all the **saints**. It is most commonly prayed aloud as the **Blessed Sacrament** is reposed after **Benediction**; it is a devotional addition, not a formal part of the **rite**.

Dix, Gregory (1901–1952)   British Anglican monk and liturgist, and author of *The Shape of the Liturgy*, among other works. It was in this work that the **fourfold structure** of the **Liturgy of the Eucharist** (take, bless, break, give) was first discussed.

Doctor of the Church   A title given to certain **saints** whose writings or **preaching** are outstanding for guiding and instructing the faithful. Ambrose, Augustine, **Gregory the Great**, and Jerome are considered the four great Doctors of the West; Athanasius, Basil the Great, Gregory Nazianzen, and **John Chrysostom** are considered the four great Doctors of the East; Thomas Aquinas is known as the Universal Doctor. There are many others, including four women— Catherine of Siena, Teresa of Avila, Thérèse of Lisieux, and Hildegard of Bingen.

Domus Dei   Term meaning "house of God" (on earth), referring to a **church** building as a place set aside for the **worship** of God.

Domus Ecclesiae   Term meaning "house of the **Church**," referring to the church building as a place suited for the liturgies the Christian community **celebrates** and reflective of that community.

Douglas, Mary (1921–2007)   British anthropologist, particularly concerned with human **symbols** and the link to culture. Her work, along with that of **Victor Turner**, is foundational for the inculturation of the **liturgy**.

Doxology   A **hymn** or prayer of praise to God. The Glory to God in the Highest, said or sung at Mass, is sometimes called the Great Doxology, and the prayer "Glory to the Father, and to the Son, and to the Holy Spirit," used in the **Rosary** and the **Liturgy of the Hours**, is sometimes called the Minor Doxology. Endings to certain prayers are also called doxologies if "praise" or "glory" are mentioned, such as the conclusion to the **Eucharistic Prayer** ("Through him, and with him, and in him . . . ") and the **Lord's Prayer** at **Mass** ("For the kingdom, the power and the glory are yours now and for ever").

Dulia   Honor given to holy men and women now in God's presence in heaven. Prayers and devotions to **saints** are dulia rather than **latria**, the **worship** given to God alone. Honor given to the Blessed Virgin Mary is called **hyperdulia**.

Easter   The commemoration of the Resurrection of the **Lord**, **celebrated** on the first **Sunday** after the first full moon after the vernal equinox. The earliest date that Easter can fall is March 22, and the latest is April 25. The celebration of Easter continues for fifty days, a period called **Easter Time**, and concludes with Evening Prayer on **Pentecost** Sunday.

Easter Candle   Another name for the **Paschal candle**.

Easter Proclamation   Another name for the **Exsultet**.

Easter Triduum   Another name for the **Paschal Triduum**.

Easter Time   The period of fifty days from the **Easter Vigil** until the conclusion of **Evening Prayer** on **Pentecost**. This **liturgical time** is **celebrated** with great joy and exultation as one great feast day, one great **Sunday** characterized especially by the singing of **Alleluia**.

Easter Vigil   The **liturgy celebrated** during the night before **Easter Sunday**; it begins after nightfall and ends before daybreak on the Sunday. The Vigil has four parts. The first part is the solemn beginning of the Vigil, or **lucernarium**. It includes the ancient practice of **blessing** a new fire and lighting the **Paschal candle**, followed by a **procession** and then the **proclamation** of Christ's Resurrection in the solemn **Exsultet**. The second part is an extended **Liturgy of the Word** where nine readings are **proclaimed**, seven from the Old Testament and two from the New Testament (the **Epistle** and the **Gospel**). The third part is the **Baptismal Liturgy** where the **elect** are baptized and confirmed and where all present renew their baptismal promises and are sprinkled with blessed

water. The last part is the **Liturgy of the Eucharist** during which the newly baptized receive **Holy Communion** for the first time. St. Augustine called it "the mother of all vigils."

Ecce Agnus Dei **Latin** for "Behold the **Lamb of God**." Immediately before the reception of **Holy Communion**, the **priest** shows the **host** to the people while saying, "Behold the Lamb of God, behold him who takes away the sins of the world. Blessed are those called to the supper of the Lamb."

Ecclesia de Eucharistia Encyclical of Pope John Paul II on the **Eucharist** and its relationship to the Church, issued April 17, 2003. In the letter the pope sought to rekindle a sense of amazement as the **Church** recognizes the **presence of Christ**. Major sections of the letter deal with the Eucharist as the **Mystery** of Faith, how the Eucharist builds the Church, the apostolicity of the Eucharist and of the Church, the Eucharist and **ecclesial** communion, the dignity of the Eucharistic celebration, and Mary as woman of the Eucharist.

Ecclesial An adjective used for anything that has to do with the **Church**.

Ecclesiology A theology of the **Church**. An implicit ecclesiology is evident in any celebration of the **liturgy**, in that liturgy manifests the reality of the Church. Certain liturgical forms help to reinforce and perpetuate certain ecclesiological models.

Economy A term derived from the Greek word for *household management*. It is used to refer to God's plan of salvation, especially as referred to by Paul in Ephesians 3:9. The divine economy is **proclaimed** and **celebrated** in the **liturgy**.

Editio Typica See **typical edition**.

Efficacy The effectiveness or fruitfulness of a **sacrament** in the life of a Christian.

Egeria (c. 350–c. 400)   A visitor to Jerusalem, possibly a Spanish nun, between the years 381 and 384, while **Cyril of Jerusalem** was bishop. She left a detailed account of the **liturgy** as **celebrated** in Jerusalem in that era, particularly the **rites** of **Holy Week**. Her name is sometimes spelled "Etheria."

Elect   Catechumens who have been formally called, or elected, by the **Church** for **Baptism**, **Confirmation**, and **Eucharist** at the next **Easter Vigil**. This election is declared at the **Rite of Election**, usually by the **bishop**, after those who have ministered to the catechumens testify regarding their readiness. The elect then enter into the final period of preparation for initiation, called **Purification and Enlightenment**.

Elements   A common term used to refer to the **bread** and the **wine** at Mass.

Elevation   The lifting up of the Eucharistic **bread** and **chalice** during the celebration of **Mass** by the **priest**, from the **Latin** *elevare*. There are four liftings or elevations during the Mass, clearly differentiated in the **rubrics** of the **Missal** and in the *General Instruction of the Roman Missal*. The first occurs during the **preparation of the gifts**, when first the **paten** with the bread and then the chalice with the **wine** are held slightly above the **altar**. The second occurs after the **consecration** of bread and wine individually, when each element is held out toward the people in a gesture of showing, not raised high (since the word *elevare* does not appear in the text at this point). The third gesture, which occurs in conjunction with the **doxology**, is a high elevation, a lifting of the **offerings** to God in the culmination of the **Eucharistic Prayer**. The fourth raising of the **elements** occurs immediately before the reception of **Holy Communion**, when the priest shows the **host**, held either over the **paten** or over the **chalice**, to the people while saying, "Behold the **Lamb of God** . . . " Similar to the showing after the consecration, this gesture is an extension of the elements toward the people, inviting them to communion. *Elevare* also is used to describe how the ***Book of the Gospels*** is carried in the **entrance procession** and the Gospel procession.

Ember Days   In the pre-1969 **liturgical calendar**, days of prayer and **fasting** scheduled in prescribed weeks during the four natural **seasons** of the year. During these days, the **Church** asked the **Lord** for particular needs and gave thanks to God publicly. In the present day, conferences of **bishops** are to arrange the time and manner of celebrating Ember Days for contemporary situations.

Embolism   An insertion of additional language into a text. It normally refers to the expansion of the **Lord's Prayer** during the **Mass**, "Deliver us, Lord, we pray, from every evil . . . " to which the people respond "For the kingdom, the power and the glory are yours now and for ever."

Enrollment of Names   Another name for the **Rite of Election**.

Entrance Antiphon   A text almost always taken from **Sacred Scripture** that is sung or said at the very beginning of **Mass**, usually during the **entrance procession**. It is sometimes referred to as the **Introit**. The entrance antiphon is given in *The Roman Missal*. Originally the antiphon began and concluded a **psalm** that was **chanted** during the entrance, which is still an option in the current Roman Missal.

Entrance Chant   Another name for the **entrance antiphon**.

Entrance Procession   The formal liturgical movement of the **priest** and **ministers** to the **sanctuary** at the beginning of **Mass**.

Environment and Art in Catholic Worship   A 1978 statement of the **Bishops'** Committee on the **Liturgy** (now the **Bishops' Committee on Divine Worship**) that speaks about principles to be considered in the preparation of liturgical space. The quality, appropriateness, and authenticity of all things used in the liturgy are also discussed. The document was superseded by ***Built of Living Stones: Art, Architecture, and Worship***, issued in 2000, which was produced by the entire Bishops' Conference.

Ephphetha   A rite of opening the ears and the mouth, associated with the celebration of **Baptism**. The rite, which has its origin in Mark 7:31–37, Jesus' healing of a deaf man, prays that the one being baptized may hear and profess the faith. It is an optional rite; it may be performed with **adults** as part of their preparation on **Holy Saturday** for initiation at the **Easter Vigil** or as part of the **Rite of Baptism for Children**, after the presentation of the lighted **candle**.

Epiclesis   A Greek word derived from the verb "to call upon" or "to invoke." *Epiclesis* can refer to any **petition** or request, but it is most commonly used to refer to the section of the **Eucharistic Prayer** that asks the Holy Spirit to come upon the **bread** and **wine** and on the community. In *The Roman Missal*, two epicleses can be discerned in most of the Eucharistic Prayers, one called a consecratory epiclesis (before the **Institution Narrative**) and the other called a communion epiclesis (after the **anamnesis**). Liturgical theology stresses the relationship between anamnesis (remembering) and epiclesis (invoking) and sees the link as a fundamental structure for all Christian prayer and sacramental activity.

Epiphany   Derived from the Greek word for "manifestation" or "appearing." The **Solemnity of the Epiphany of the Lord** commemorates the visit of the Magi to the newborn **Christ** child and, thus, the first manifestation or revelation of Jesus to the non-Jewish world. Traditionally **celebrated** on January 6, in the United States and some other countries, it is celebrated on the **Sunday** between January 2 and January 8 inclusive.

Epistle   An older word for "letter," derived from Greek and **Latin**. The word most commonly refers to the New Testament letters of Paul, John, and others. The **second reading** at **Masses** that have two readings before the **Gospel** is sometimes referred to as the Epistle since it is usually, though not exclusively, drawn from one of those letters.

Eucharist The **sacrament** whereby **Christ** becomes truly, completely, and permanently present under the appearances of **bread** and **wine**. The entire action of celebrating the **sacrifice** of the **Mass** is commonly called the Eucharist, as are the **consecrated elements**. The word is derived from the Greek for "**thanksgiving**"; it was used as early as in the *Didache* and by St. **Justin** (c. 100–c. 165).

Eucharistic Fast The practice of refraining from food and drink before the reception of **Holy Communion**. The purpose is to create a spiritual hunger and to emphasize that the **Eucharist** is not ordinary food and that its consumption is a sacred act. Current **Church** law prescribes that a person who is going to receive Holy Communion must refrain from food or drink for one hour before Holy Communion, with the exceptions of **water** and medicine. The sick and elderly are exempt.

Eucharistic Prayer The central prayer of the **Mass**. It is an act of **thanksgiving**, praise, **blessing**, and **consecration**. It corresponds to Jesus' act of blessing during the **Last Supper**, the second of the **fourfold actions** of taking, blessing, breaking, and giving by which the **Eucharist** is often described. The Eucharistic Prayer is the **form** of the **sacrament**; the words of **Christ** ("This is my Body . . . this is the **chalice** of my Blood . . . ") are essential. In Greek-speaking **churches** it is called the **anaphora**. Scholars suggest that the Eucharistic Prayer may have developed from the *birkat ha-mazon*, the Jewish grace after meals.

The Eucharistic Prayer includes a thanksgiving to God for the work of salvation, an **acclamation**, the **Sanctus**, an **epiclesis**, the **Institution Narrative** and **consecration**, the **anamnesis**, the **oblation** or offering of the **memorial** to God, together with the **sacrifice** of the **assembly**, the **intercessions**, prayers for the whole **Church**, and the final **doxology**.

Eucharistic Prayer for Masses with Children   Three
Eucharistic Prayers provided for use at Masses where preadolescent
children make up the majority of participants. Although they do
not appear in the third (current) edition of *The Roman Missal*,
they have been adapted for use with the current edition and are
published by the conferences of bishops of the United States and
some other English-speaking countries.

Eucharistic Prayer for Reconciliation   Two of the Eucharistic
Prayers given in *The Roman Missal* have the title "Eucharistic
Prayer for Reconciliation." These prayers may appropriately be
used in any time of conflict or division, as well as in Lent, when
the mystery of our reconciliation in Christ is also central.

Eucharistic Prayer for Use in Masses for Various Needs
One of the Eucharistic Prayers given in *The Roman Missal*.
The one prayer actually has four different sets of prefaces and
intercessions based on four different themes, and so has four forms.
The first has the theme "The Church on the Path of Unity"; the
second has the theme "God Guides His Church along the Way of
Salvation"; the third is "Jesus, the Way to the Father"; the fourth is
"Jesus, Who Went About Doing Good." They are intended to be
paired with the Masses and Prayers for Various Needs and
Occasions in *The Roman Missal*.

Eucharistic Procession   A solemn procession in which the
Eucharist is carried, often through the streets, to give public witness
of faith and devotion toward the Blessed Sacrament. This occurs
most often on the Solemnity of the Most Holy Body and Blood of
Christ. The ritual book *Holy Communion and Worship of the
Eucharist outside Mass* gives the norms and rubrics for
Eucharistic processions.

Eucharistic Reservation   The practice of keeping the **bread** of the **Eucharist** in the **tabernacle**. The primary and original reason for reservation is the administration of **Viaticum**; it is also for the **adoration** of our **Lord** and for the giving of **Holy Communion** outside **Mass**, particularly to the sick and homebound. The practice stems from the Catholic belief that the **Real Presence** of the Lord remains permanently after **consecration**.

Eucharistic Sacrifice   The **Mass**.

Eucharistic Species   One or both of the **elements** of **bread** and **wine** that have been **consecrated** and have become the Body and Blood of **Christ**.

Euchology   A term derived from the Greek word for "prayer." It usually refers to a collection of prayers or to the texts used in a **liturgy**. A book containing prayers is sometimes called a *euchologion*.

Eulogy   A speech given in praise of a person or thing, most often in praise of a recently deceased person. The *Order of Christian Funerals* allows that a family member or friend may offer words of remembrance before the concluding **rite** at the **Vigil Service** for the deceased and/or at the beginning of the **Final Commendation** at the **Funeral Mass**. These words of remembrance are different from a eulogy; they recall the life of the deceased in a faith context, whereas a eulogy is traditionally focused on praising the individual or recounting anecdotes of the person's life. Both are different from the **homily**, which should focus on the Scriptures **proclaimed** and on the participation of the dead person in the **Paschal Mystery**.

Evangeliary   The *Book of the Gospels*.

Evangelization and Precatechumenate   The first period or stage in the process described in the *Rite of Christian Initiation of Adults*. During this time, **adults** who express an interest in the faith are introduced to **Christ** through the **Gospel** and the **Church**. People in this stage may be referred to as **inquirers**. The period ends with the **Rite** of Acceptance into the **Order** of **Catechumens**.

Evening Mass of the Lord's Supper   A common name given to the **Mass of the Lord's Supper celebrated** on **Holy Thursday**.

Evening Prayer   One of the two primary **canonical hours** of the **Liturgy of the Hours**, (along with **Morning Prayer**); also called **Vespers**. In the present **Roman Rite**, it consists of the introductory verse, a **hymn**, psalmody (two **psalms** and a **canticle**), a reading from Scripture with its **responsory**, the **Canticle of Mary**, **intercessions**, Our Father, and a concluding prayer and **blessing**. Evening Prayer reflects on the graces given and the work accomplished during the day; it also recalls redemption and, as daylight fades, prompts the Christian to ask God for the grace of eternal light in **Christ**.

Examination of Conscience   An action by which an individual reviews his or her life over a period of time in an attempt to call to mind sinful actions, often measured against the Ten Commandments and the teachings of **Christ** and the **Church**. An examination of conscience may also take place as a communal and liturgical act; in the *Rite of Penance*, it takes place after the **homily** in the Rite of **Reconciliation** of Several Penitents with Individual **Confession**. A brief examination of conscience is also customary at the beginning of **Night Prayer**.

Ex Opere Operantis   **Latin** for "by the action of the one acting." The term refers to the fruitfulness of a sacramental action by considering the subjective holiness or disposition of the **minister** or the one receiving the **sacrament**. The grace conveyed in a sacrament may be received in vain, or fruitlessly, if the recipient is not properly disposed. Even so, in Catholic theology *ex opere operantis* is secondary to ***ex opere operato***.

Ex Opere Operato   Latin for "by the action having been done." The term refers to the **efficacy** of a sacramental action by considering the objective fact of the **ritual** being performed properly. A more precise understanding of sacramental efficacy is gained when *ex opere operato* is understood in tandem with ***ex opere operantis*** *Christi*: a sacramental action ultimately depends on the action of **Christ** for its efficacy, and Christ has guaranteed his presence and grace, regardless of the faith and holiness of the human individuals involved.

Exorcism   A prayer or command given to cast out the presence of the devil. The ***Rite of Baptism for Children*** contains a prayer of exorcism, which takes place after the **Litany of the Saints**. The ***Rite of Christian Initiation of Adults*** contains prayers of exorcism as part of the **rites** belonging to the period of the **catechumenate** and as part of the **scrutinies**. There is a Rite of Exorcism for use in the case of possession; it may be used only with the express permission of a **bishop** and only by mandated **priest**-exorcists.

Explanatory Rites   Rites that take place immediately after a sacramental action that serve to amplify the meaning and effects of the **sacrament**. In the **Baptism** of **children**, for example, the **anointing** with **chrism** after Baptism, the clothing with a **white garment**, the giving of the lighted **candle**, and the **ephphetha** prayer are all explanatory rites.

Exposition of the Blessed Sacrament   A liturgical **ritual** that includes **hymns**, prayers, and readings from Scripture during which the reserved **Blessed Sacrament** is removed from the **tabernacle** and placed on the **altar**, either in a closed **ciborium** or exposed in a **monstrance**, for the faithful to adore. The **rite** is an acknowledgment of **Christ's Real Presence** in the **Eucharist** and is meant to foster a spirit of deeper participation in the **offering** of the **sacrifice** at **Mass**.

The **rite** may conclude with the rite of **Benediction of the Blessed Sacrament**.

Exsultet   The solemn proclamation of the Resurrection of Christ that is sung at the **Easter Vigil** after the **procession** with the newly lit **Paschal candle**. Ideally it is sung by a **deacon**, although it may also be sung by the priest **celebrant**, or a concelebrating priest, or a lay **cantor**. The Exsultet derives its name from the first word of the **Latin** text, "rejoice." The authorship of the Exsultet is unknown, but tradition sometimes attributes this great poem of praise to Ambrose or Augustine.

Extraordinary Form of the Mass   The **Mass celebrated** according to *The Roman Missal* promulgated after the **Council of Trent** as updated in 1962 by **Pope John XXIII**; sometimes referred to as the **Tridentine Mass**. The term originated with Pope Benedict XVI in his 2007 apostolic letter *Summorum Pontificum*. The term distinguishes this celebration of the Mass from the **ordinary form**.

Extraordinary Minister of Holy Communion   The liturgical **minister** who is authorized by the **bishop** to assist **priests** and **deacons** in the distribution of **Holy Communion**. An extraordinary minister functions when a sufficient number of **ordinary ministers** is not present.

Extreme Unction   The name used before the revision of the **sacraments** after the Second Vatican Council for the **sacrament** now called the **Anointing of the Sick**. This former name emphasizes the previous common practice of delaying the reception of the sacrament until the moment of death, so that it was truly the last (*extreme*) **anointing** (*unction*).

Faculty   A right granted to enable a person to do something. For example, the *General Instruction of the Roman Missal* gives **priests** the faculty to **celebrate** or concelebrate Mass more than once a day in particular circumstances; it also gives **bishops** the faculty to permit communion under both kinds on occasions not listed in the GIRM. Priests normally request from the local bishop the faculty to exercise public ministry when not in their home diocese.

Faldstool   From a German word meaning "folding stool or chair." The word refers to the chair a **bishop** uses when he is not seated at his **cathedra**, but in front of the **altar** for visibility during certain special **rites**. It can also refer to the chair a bishop uses outside the **cathedral church**.

Fasting   The custom of not eating food or certain foods, or of eating a reduced quantity of food. It is mentioned in Scripture (see Matthew 6:16–18) and was practiced by Jesus during the forty days in the desert after his **baptism**. See also **abstinence**.

Fathers of the Church   Collective term for the great writers and preachers of the early **Church**, generally the first six centuries. Their writings reflect a unified approach to theology, discussing aspects of the faith not according to different disciplines, but as a whole. The **second reading** in the **Office of Readings** is often taken from one of the Fathers.

Feast   A rank within the category of liturgical days, lower than a **solemnity** but higher than a **memorial**. Feasts usually do not include **Evening Prayer** I, but usually do have a complete **proper** set of texts for the **Mass** along with readings.

Feria   The **Latin** word for "weekday." It refers to a day on which there is no **solemnity**, **feast**, or **obligatory memorial** assigned.

Fermentum   Historically, the particle of the Eucharistic **bread consecrated** by the pope and taken by **deacons** and other **ministers** to various **Masses** held elsewhere in the city of Rome. The *fermentum* was then dropped into the **chalice** during the **commingling** as a **sign** of unity of the local gathering with the papal celebration.

Final Blessing   A **blessing** given at the conclusion of a **liturgy**. It may take the form of a simple blessing, a **solemn blessing**, or a **prayer over the people**.

Final Commendation   The concluding **rite** of the **Funeral Mass** or of the Funeral **Liturgy** outside Mass. The rite, which replaces the usual **Concluding Rites** of a Mass, includes the song of farewell, during which an **incensation** and sprinkling of the body may take place; the Prayer of Commendation; and the **dismissal** to the place of committal. The Final Commendation may also be **celebrated** at the place of committal, usually a cemetery or mausoleum.

First Friday   A devotion that grew out of the promises said to have been made by **Christ** in an apparition to St. Margaret Mary Alacoque in the late 1600s. They assured special graces in life and at the moment of death to those who **consecrate** the first Friday of each month to the Sacred Heart of Jesus. The observance centers on attendance at **Mass** and receiving **Holy Communion** on the first Fridays of nine consecutive months. It is customary but not required that a **Votive Mass** of the Sacred Heart be said on First Fridays.

First Reading   The first Scripture reading during the **Liturgy of the Word**. On **Sundays** and other important days, it is usually taken from the Old Testament, or, during **Easter Time**, from the Acts of the Apostles or Revelation. On weekdays, it may be taken from either the Old Testament or the New Testament writings of the **Apostles**, but not from the **Gospels**.

First Saturday   The devotion centering around attending **Mass** and receiving **Holy Communion** on the first Saturdays of five consecutive months in honor of Mary, the Mother of the **Lord**. This devotion grew rapidly after the apparition of Mary at Fatima in 1917.

First Vespers   Another name for **Evening Prayer** I, which begins the observance of a **Sunday** or **solemnity, celebrated** on the preceding evening.

Fixed Altar   An **altar** that is attached to the floor. Every **church** should have a fixed altar to signify **Christ** as the living stone (see 1 Peter 2:4; Ephesians 2:20).

Flagon   A pitcher that is used to hold the **wine** that is carried forward in the **procession with the gifts**. Ideally, it is large enough to hold all the wine to be **consecrated** as a **sign** of the **assembly**'s unity in the Eucharistic celebration. The wine is to be poured from the flagon into chalices during the **preparation of the gifts**.

Font   Another name for the **Baptismal Font**.

Form   The text or formula that constitutes the major verbal aspect of a **sacrament**. Form is frequently linked to **matter** in a sacramental **rite**. Thus the form of **Baptism**, "I baptize you in the Name of the Father, and of the Son, and of the Holy Spirit," derived from the end of the **Gospel** of Matthew, is spoken as the person being baptized is immersed or **water** is poured by the **minister** of the sacrament.

Fourfold Eucharistic Actions   The actions of taking, blessing, breaking, and giving. These are the actions that Jesus performed at table at the **Last Supper**, the actions the **Church** continues to do in obedience to the **Lord's** command to "Do this in memory of me," and the actions by which we recognize the Lord's presence among us. By these same actions, the disciples on the way to Emmaus recognized the risen **Christ** in their midst, and the same fourfold actions are mentioned in the accounts of the feeding miracles in the Gospels. The Church ritualizes these actions in the **preparation of the gifts** (take), the **Eucharistic Prayer** (bless), the **fraction of the Bread** (break), and **Holy Communion** (give).

Fraction of the Bread   The **ritual** action of dividing the common loaf of Eucharistic **bread** into many pieces to be distributed at **Holy Communion**. In the **Roman Rite** this takes place after the recitation of the **Lord's Prayer** and the **sign of peace**, and before the invitation to participate in Holy Communion. It signifies that the many faithful are made one body by partaking of the one loaf (see 1 Corinthians 10:17).

Friday of the Passion of the Lord (Good Friday)   The day within the **Paschal Triduum** that commemorates the Death of the Lord Jesus **Christ** on the **Cross**. The principal **liturgy** is the **Celebration of the Passion of the Lord**. It is a day of **fasting** and **abstinence**, and by ancient tradition, the **Church** does not **celebrate** the **sacraments** on this day, except for **Penance** and **Anointing of the Sick**. The day should be marked with sobriety and prayer in the life of a Christian.

Frontal   An ornamental cloth, frequently in the **liturgical color** of the celebration, that may hang in front of the **altar** or **ambo**, facing the **assembly**; also called an **antependium**.

Funeral Mass The principal liturgical celebration of the Christian community for the deceased. The **liturgy** begins with the **greeting** at the **church** entrance of the mourners who accompany the deceased, a sprinkling of the coffin with **holy water**, and the placing of the funeral **pall** on the coffin. After the **entrance procession**, a Christian **symbol** may be placed on the coffin. After the **collect**, the **Liturgy of the Word** and the **Liturgy of the Eucharist** are **celebrated** in the usual manner, and the **Mass** concludes with the **Final Commendation**. In the case of a funeral liturgy outside Mass, the Liturgy of the Word is celebrated and Final Commendation follows the **Universal Prayer** and the Our Father.

G

Gathering in the Presence of the Body   One of the **rites** in the *Order of Christian Funerals*. This is a simple rite that can be used when the family gathers in the presence of the body for the first time, when the body is to be prepared for burial, or any time after it has been prepared. It includes a brief Scripture reading, a sprinkling of the body with **holy water**, a **psalm**, the **Lord's Prayer**, and concluding prayer and **blessing**.

Gathering Space   Another name for the **narthex** in a **church**.

Gaudete Sunday   Name given to the Third Sunday of **Advent**, taken from the first word of the **entrance antiphon** in **Latin**, *Gaudete*, "rejoice." **Rose**-colored **vestments** may be worn on this day instead of **violet**.

Gelineau, Joseph (1920–2008)   French Jesuit liturgist particularly noted for his contribution to the modern appreciation of liturgical music. He is known for composing **psalm** tones that allow the psalms to be sung according to the Hebrew patterns of syllabic stresses. In English, his psalm tones are commonly used with the Grail translation of the psalms. He was a consultor to the commission (**Consilium**) for the revision of the **Order** of **Mass** following the Second Vatican Council.

General Instruction of the Liturgy of the Hours   The introductory document, or **praenotanda**, that explains the theological background and gives directions for celebrating the **Liturgy of the Hours**. It is found at the beginning of the first volume of the *Liturgy of the Hours*.

General Instruction of the Roman Missal (GIRM) The introductory document, or ***praenotanda***, that explains the theological background and gives the directions for celebrating the **Mass**. It appears at the beginning of *The Roman Missal*, and it is published separately.

Genuflection A gesture of respect and adoration. In this gesture, the right knee touches the ground while the left knee is bent and the upper body is erect. It was borrowed by Western Christianity from the secular gestures of respect to civil authorities. It is unknown in many Eastern **Churches**. A single genuflection on one knee is the proper gesture before the **Blessed Sacrament** whether it is on the **altar** at Mass, reserved in the **tabernacle**, or exposed for adoration. The double genuflection, on both knees, has been discontinued.

Gift Table The table located in the midst of the **assembly** on which the **gifts** of **bread** and **wine** are placed before they are carried in **procession** to the **altar** at the beginning of the **Liturgy of the Eucharist**.

Gifts The **elements** of **bread** and **wine** to be **consecrated** to become the Body and Blood of **Christ**. The gifts may also be referred to as the **offerings**.

Gloria in Excelsis The song of praise, which in English begins with the words "Glory to God in the highest," sung on certain prescribed days as part of the **Introductory Rites** of the **Mass**. It is based on the **hymn** of the **angels** at **Christ**'s birth (see Luke 2:14).

Godparents Members of the Christian community, chosen for their good example and their close relationship to the one being baptized, who are present at the celebration of **Baptism** and provide guidance and assistance to the one baptized afterward. In the case of **adult** Baptism, godparents assist with the final preparation and formation of the **catechumens** and at the **Rite of Election** testify to their readiness for initiation. In the Baptism of **children**, godparents assist the parents in raising the child in the faith and, at the celebration, profess the **Church's** faith with the parents. To be a godparent, a Catholic must have received all three **sacraments of initiation** and be living a life consistent with Catholic teaching. Only one godparent is required at Baptism, but if there are two, one is to be a male and one a female. A baptized non-Catholic may act as a **Christian witness** along with a Catholic godparent.

Gold　In the dioceses of the United States of America, **vestments** of gold color may be worn at **Mass** in place of **white** vestments on more solemn occasions.

Good Friday　Another name for **Friday of the Passion of the Lord**.

Gospel　The good news of Jesus **Christ**. The term *Gospel* usually refers to one of the four accounts of the life, death, and Resurrection of Jesus found in the **Bible**, ascribed to Matthew, Mark, Luke, and John.

Gospel Acclamation　The title given to the **rite** within the celebration of **Mass** that greets the **Lord** who is about to speak to the **assembly** in the **Gospel** and prepares the assembly for its proclamation. The Gospel Acclamation consists of the **Alleluia** (or, during **Lent**, other words of praise) sung by all, followed by a verse (frequently from Scripture) sung by a **cantor** or by the **choir**, and then the refrain sung again by all. Several verses may be used to cover the action of a **Gospel procession**.

Gospel Canticle　The **hymn** that is sung or recited after the reading and its **responsory** at **Morning Prayer**, **Evening Prayer**, and **Night Prayer**. At Morning Prayer, the Gospel Canticle is the **Canticle of Zechariah**; at Evening Prayer it is the **Canticle of Mary**; at Night Prayer it is the **Canticle of Simeon**. The Gospel Canticles are treated with the same dignity that is given to the **proclamation** of the **Gospel** at **Mass**; hence, participants stand to sing or recite the canticle, and sign themselves with the **Sign of the Cross** at the beginning of each one.

Gospel Procession   The name for the **procession** of the **deacon** or **priest** to the **ambo** for the proclamation of the **Gospel**. The **minister** takes the *Book of the Gospels* and processes with it from the **altar** to the ambo during the singing of the **Gospel Acclamation**. He may be preceded by a **thurifer** and/or by ministers with **candles**.

Gradual   A name used at times to refer to the **psalm** sung or **proclaimed** after the **first reading** at **Mass**.

Graduale Romanum   The *Roman Gradual*, the liturgical book that contains the **chants** of the **Mass**, along with their musical notation. Both the **ordinary** and the **proper** of the Mass are contained in this book.

Graduale Simplex   The *Simple Gradual*, a liturgical book that contains simpler **chants** to be sung in place of the more complex melodies found in the *Graduale Romanum*.

Great Entrance   The solemn transfer of the prepared **bread** and **wine** from the side table to the **altar** during a **Byzantine Rite** Eucharistic **liturgy**. During the Great Entrance, the Cherubic Hymn is sung, which is interrupted by commemorations sung by the clergy. After the Great Entrance there follows a **litany**, the **kiss of peace**, the **Nicene Creed**, and then the **Eucharistic Prayer**.

Green   The **liturgical color** used during **Ordinary Time**.

Greeter   A liturgical **minister** who welcomes individuals as they arrive at a **church** for **worship**. In many parishes, **ushers** also perform the ministry of greeter. Sometimes they are referred to as **ministers of hospitality**.

Greeting   A brief, formalized dialogue using **ritual** language usually expressing a wish of God's grace or presence to another, including a standardized response by the one(s) being greeted, for example, "The grace of our **Lord** Jesus **Christ**, and the love of God, and the communion of the Holy Spirit be with you all" to which the people respond with the words, "And with your spirit." The liturgical greeting should not be replaced or embellished with secular greetings such as "Good morning" since it is ritual language seeking the presence of God.

Gregorian Chant   A form of **chant**, named after Pope **Gregory the Great**, that does not employ any harmonies. It has been used for centuries in the celebration of **Mass** in the Roman **Church**.

Gregory the Great (540–604)   Pope and liturgical reformer. Many prayers composed by him are found in a collection called the Gregorian **Sacramentary**. Among other achievements, he revived the practice of **stational Masses**, prescribed that the **Alleluia** be used outside of **Lent**, emphasized the **homily**, and moved the **Lord's Prayer** to its present location after the **Eucharistic Prayer** in the **Roman Rite**.

Gremial   A linen apron used by a **bishop** to protect the **chasuble** when oil is being used, for example, when the hands of the newly-ordained are **anointed** with **chrism**. In common practice, an **amice** is often used as a gremial.

Guardini, Romano (1885–1968)   Italian-born liturgist who spent most of his life in Germany. Author of *The Spirit of the Liturgy*, among other important books; he was one of the first to introduce the "dialogue" **Mass** (in **Latin**) in the late 1920s in his youth center, and rearranged the **chapel** to allow Mass facing the **congregation**, which was seated on three sides of the **altar** area. He held a chair at the University of Munich.

Guéranger, Prosper (1805–1875)   Founder of the restored Benedictine Abbey at **Solesmes** (1832). He is considered the founder of the modern **liturgical movement** because he sought to reconnect **liturgy** with the life of the people.

H

Hail Mary   A common prayer used in devotion to Mary, the Mother of God. The first half of the prayer is derived from the **Gospel** of Luke; the second half is a traditional formula composed by the **Church**. The form used by the **Roman Rite** is: "Hail Mary, full of grace, the **Lord** is with you. Blessed are you among women, and blessed is the fruit of your womb, Jesus. Holy Mary, Mother of God, pray for us sinners, now and at the hour of our death. **Amen**."

Hanc Igitur   Name given to that paragraph in **Eucharistic Prayer** I that begins, "Therefore, **Lord**, we pray . . . " It is a **petition** that asks the Lord to accept the **oblation** offered by the entire **Church** ("your whole family"). Special forms of the Hanc igitur are provided for the **Mass of the Lord's Supper**, the **Easter Octave**, and most **ritual Masses**.

Head Bow   A **sign** of reverence where only the head, not the entire body, is bowed. It may be used during the liturgy at the mention of the three Divine Persons, the names of Jesus, of the Blessed Virgin Mary, and of the **saint** in whose honor the **Mass** is being **celebrated**.

Hierarchy   In general, any sort of arrangement in which there are different levels of structure or organization.

The liturgical **assembly** is hierarchically arrayed, or ordered, in that it is united as one body under the **bishop**. Within that body, there are different identities (for example, ordained and lay; among the ordained, the different ranks of **Holy Orders**) and functions. Within the hierarchical structure, all participate equally but not in the same way. The term itself comes from a Greek word meaning "rank," but in current use does not mean that one level is "higher" in the sense of being holier or more important, although the word is often mistakenly used in that way. In popular parlance, the term "**hierarchy**" is often used to refer solely to the bishops and other administrators, or to the clergy alone.

High Church   A term used to describe those communities that practice a style of **liturgy** that emphasizes **ritual** and sacramental **rites**. The Roman Catholic and Orthodox **Churches** are considered the major high churches, along with certain segments of the Anglican communion. To distinguish themselves from high churches, some communities use the label **low church**.

Hippolytus   A Roman **presbyter** who lived in the first half of the third century. He was banished in 235 by the Emperor. The books of laws (**canons**) and the *Apostolic Tradition* (ca. 215) attributed to him provide valuable information on the liturgical and **ecclesial** life of the early Roman **Church**.

Holy Communion   The action of receiving the **consecrated elements** of **bread** and **wine** that have become the Body and Blood of **Christ**. The term "communion" is often used to refer to the elements themselves—for example, "receiving communion."

Holy Communion and Worship of the Eucharist outside Mass   The **ritual** book that gives the norms and **rubrics** for the distribution of **Holy Communion** outside Mass, and the rites for the **worship** of the **Eucharist** outside **Mass**. The rubrics for **Exposition** and **Benediction of the Blessed Sacrament** can be found here as well as information concerning **Eucharistic processions** and Eucharistic Congresses.

Holy Communion under Both Kinds   The practice of offering to the entire **assembly** Holy Communion under both **species** or forms, that is, both the **consecrated bread**, which is always offered, and the consecrated **wine**. The reception of the consecrated wine by the assembly had fallen into disuse for several centuries but was again authorized by the Second Vatican Council.

Holy, Holy, Holy   The English name for the **Sanctus**, that is, the **preface acclamation** which forms part of the **Eucharistic Prayer** and begins with the words, "Holy, Holy, Holy **Lord** God of **hosts**."

Holy Oils   The collective name for the **oil of catechumens**, the **oil of the sick**, and the sacred **chrism**, **blessed** and **consecrated** by the **bishop** on or near **Holy Thursday** and distributed to the parishes for use in the **sacraments**.

Holy Orders   The **sacrament** by which men are ordained for ministry in the **Church** as **deacons**, **priests**, or **bishops**. The sacrament is conferred through the **Rite** of **Ordination**, which includes the **laying on of hands** (the **matter**) by a bishop on the **candidate**, followed by the Prayer of Ordination (the **form**) particular to each order.

Holy Saturday   The Saturday within the **Paschal Triduum**. It is a day marked by meditation, prayer, and **fasting** in anticipation of the Resurrection of the **Lord**. As on **Good Friday**, no **sacraments** are **celebrated** on this day except for **Penance** and the **Anointing** of the Sick, in cases of need. Communion may be given only as **Viaticum**. **Mass** is not celebrated until the **Easter Vigil**, which takes place after sunset on Saturday night. Several **Preparation Rites** for the **elect** who will be receiving the **sacraments of initiation** at the **Vigil** are proper to this day.

Holy Thursday   Another name for **Thursday of the Lord's Supper**, or **Thursday of Holy Week**.

Holy Water   Water that has been **blessed**. Holy water is usually found in **stoups**, or **fonts**, at the entrances of **churches** so that individuals may bless themselves with it, reminding them of the waters of **Baptism**. It is also used when **blessing** objects and people. In many churches, a large, covered container of holy water is kept so that the faithful may take some home for devotional use.

Holy Week   The week from **Palm Sunday of the Passion of the Lord** through **Easter Sunday**, which commemorates **Christ**'s last days on earth, and **celebrates** the **Paschal Mystery** of his Death and Resurrection.

Holyday of Obligation   Solemn feasts marked by attendance at **Mass** and by refraining from unnecessary work as much as possible. The exact days vary from country to country. In the United States, the holydays of obligation are January 1, the **Solemnity** of Mary, the Holy Mother of God; the Solemnity of the Ascension; August 15, the Solemnity of the Assumption of the Blessed Virgin Mary; November 1, the Solemnity of All **Saints**; December 8, the Solemnity of the Immaculate Conception of the Blessed Virgin Mary; and December 25, the Solemnity of the Nativity of Our **Lord** Jesus **Christ** (**Christmas**). In Canada, Christmas and the Solemnity of Mary, the Mother of God, are holydays of obligation.

Homily   An explanation of the Scripture readings or other text from the **Mass** being **celebrated**, usually after the **proclamation** of the **Gospel**. It is also a reflection on the implications of Scripture and a challenge to the **assembly** to conversion and renewal. By canonical definition (**canon 767 §1** of the 1983 *Code of Canon Law*) the homily at Mass is reserved to the ordained. At **Mass**, the homily is ordinarily given by the **celebrant**, although it may be entrusted to a concelebrating **priest** or to the **deacon**. A homily is integrally related to the **liturgy** being celebrated. In differs from a **sermon**, which is a thematic talk not necessarily related to the liturgical action or texts.

Hosanna   A Hebrew exclamation of joy, triumph, and praise, taken from the **psalms**, and which means, "Save us, we pray," or "May God save us." The word is used in the **Sanctus** in the **Eucharistic Prayer**, and it is also sung in the refrains of the psalms or **hymn** during the **procession** with **palms** on **Palm Sunday of the Lord's Passion**.

Host   (1) The unleavened wafer of **bread** used at the **Eucharist** in Western **churches**. It derives from the **Latin** *hostia*, meaning "sacrificial victim." The *General Instruction of the Roman Missal* urges the use of a host large enough to be broken and shared by the **priest** and at least some of the people.

(2) When used in the plural, as in "God of hosts" or "heavenly hosts," the word refers to **angels** (from the Latin *hostis*, "army").

Humeral Veil   A **vestment** consisting of a rectangle of fabric, similar to that used for a **chasuble**, about two feet by nine feet. It is worn over the shoulders and secured with a clasp over the chest so that the ends can be used to carry (and cover) something precious. It is commonly worn by the **priest** or **deacon** at **Benediction** or when carrying the **Blessed Sacrament** in a solemn **procession**. A smaller and lighter vestment, called a **vimpa**, is similar to a humeral veil and worn by the **miter bearer** and **crosier bearer** when a **bishop** celebrates.

Hymn   In the context of the **liturgy**, a religious song, the majority of which is non-Scriptural, that has become part of the **ordinary** or **proper**. For example, the **Glory to God in the Highest** is usually classified as a hymn, since, aside from the first sentence taken from Luke's **Gospel**, it is a composition developed by the Christian community. Songs taken directly from Scripture, other than **psalms**, are called **canticles**.

Hymnal   A book containing **hymns** for **worship**.

Hyperdulia   The special honor and reverence given to the Blessed Virgin Mary. It is above (in Greek, *hyper*) the honor given to the **saints** (*dulia*), but not equal to the **worship** properly given to God alone (*latria*).

I

Icon   A sacred image, painted according to traditional norms, especially associated with **Eastern Christianity**. Icons are considered to be windows into heaven, rather than mere reminders of the past. **Christ** is called the icon of the unseen God in Colossians 1:15, and the term can be applied by analogy to other things, such as the **Church** as a whole. It is also spelled *ikon* or *eikon*.

Iconastasis   The **icon** screen or solid wall separating the **sanctuary** from the body of the **church** in a **Byzantine** Church (e.g., Russian or Greek). It usually has three doorways for the clergy to pass through in the course of the **liturgy**: the central Holy or Royal Doors and the two side (**deacon**'s) doors. The icon to the right of the central doorway must be that of **Christ** and the icon to the left of the central doors must be that of Mary.

Illuminandi   "Those who will be enlightened," a name sometimes given to the **elect**. The term is used because **Baptism** has been called *illuminatio* (**enlightenment**) insofar as it fills the newly baptized with the light of faith.

In Directum   Term referring to the singing of a **psalm** straight through, especially in the **Liturgy of the Hours**. It is usually done by a soloist, soloist and **choir**, or choir alone, rarely by the **congregation**.

In Persona Christi Capitis   "In the person of **Christ** the head." The phrase refers to the **priest**'s role as he leads and presides over the **worship** of the **Church** at **liturgy**, especially the celebration of the **Eucharist**. See *Catechism of the Catholic Church*, 1142.

Immersion   The method of administering **Baptism** in which the **candidate** is totally immersed three times in a **font** or pool. In the case of an older child or adult, and based on the construction of the font or pool, the **minister** may also stand in the pool. The baptismal formula is pronounced as the immersion takes place. In *Christian Initiation*, General Introduction, 22, immersion is deemed the more suitable method for symbolizing participation in the Death and Resurrection of **Christ**.

Imposition of Hands   Another term used for the **laying on of hands**.

Incarnate   Term used in the **Niceno-Constantinopolitan Creed** ("and by the Holy Spirit was incarnate of the Virgin Mary, and became man") referring to the divine **mystery** of the taking of human nature by the Second Person of the Blessed Trinity.

Incense   Grains of resins or other natural substances that are placed on burning charcoal to produce a sweet-smelling smoke. According to **Psalm** 141:2 and Revelation 8:4, incense symbolizes prayer. It is a way to respect and honor individuals and sacred objects. The term can be used for both the grains of resins and for the smoke that is produced.

Incensation   The act of honoring an individual or an object with **incense**. This can be accomplished by a **minister** swinging the smoking **thurible** (**censer**) in front of a person, or in front of or around an object, or by allowing the smoke to rise from a **brazier** placed in front of an object.

Incense Boat   The vessel used to contain **incense** before it is burned. It can also be simply called a boat. The name derives from the customary shape of this vessel.

Indicative Form The textual form in which the **celebrant** uses "I," as in the **Roman Rite**'s common formula for **Baptism** ("I baptize you") and for sacramental **absolution** in the *Rite of Penance* ("I absolve you from your sins"). Alternative forms for such liturgical texts are called **deprecative** or **invocative**.

Indult A privilege granted in exception to a particular **Church** law by the Holy See or a **bishop** for a specific length of time.

Infusion The method of administering **Baptism** by which the **minister** pours **water** over the head of the **candidate** while pronouncing the words, "N., I baptize you in the name of the Father, and of the Son, and of the Holy Spirit." It is also called **affusion**.

Inquirer An unbaptized **adult** who is in the very first stage of the process of **Christian initiation**. Inquirers express an initial interest about becoming Catholic and show the first stirrings of faith. They begin to learn about the Christian life and are introduced to **Gospel** values. Although "inquirer" is a name given to them, it is not a formal **order** in the **Church**, and there are no liturgical **rituals** associated with this stage.

Inquiry Another name given to the period of **evangelization and precatechumenate**, the first period or stage in the process of **Christian initiation**.

Institution The formal **rite** whereby men preparing for the **Sacrament** of **Holy Orders** are installed in the ministries of **lector** and **acolyte** on a stable basis.

Institution Narrative The section of the **Eucharistic Prayer** in which the **celebrant** narrates what the **Lord** Jesus did and said at the **Last Supper** when he instituted the **Eucharist**. The traditional Catholic teaching is that when the **priest** repeats the words of **Christ** during this section of the **Eucharistic Prayer**, the **bread** and **wine** are **consecrated** and become the Body and Blood of Christ. Thus the Institution Narrative is sometimes referred to as the **Words of Institution** or the **consecration**.

Intercession (1) Appeals or requests on behalf of others—i.e., mediation. In this sense, we ask others, including **Christ**, his Mother, the **angels**, **saints**, and the **People of God** to intercede for us through their prayers and merits.

(2) One of the specific intentions or prayers that are announced in the **Universal Prayer** at **Mass** or as part of the intercessions in the **Liturgy of the Hours**.

(3) In the plural, it is the name for the section of the **Eucharistic Prayer** in which intercession is made for **Church ministers**, the living and the dead, thereby showing the unity between the local community and Christians throughout the world and throughout history.

International Commission on English in the Liturgy (ICEL)

A commission of Catholic **bishops'** conferences from countries where English is used in the celebration of the liturgy in the **Roman Rite**. Often referred to by the acronym ICEL, its purpose is to prepare English translations of the **Latin** liturgical texts under the direction of Rome. Eleven bishops' conferences are members of ICEL: Australia, Canada, England and Wales, India, Ireland, New Zealand, Pakistan, the Philippines, Scotland, Southern Africa, and the United States of America. There are an additional fifteen conferences that have associate membership.

Intinction The form of distributing **Holy Communion under both kinds** in which a **minister** dips a particle of the **consecrated bread** into a **chalice** containing the consecrated **wine**. The particle is then placed directly in the **communicant**'s mouth; reception of Holy Communion in the hand is not possible when intinction is used. Although allowed by law, it is a less preferred manner for distributing Holy Communion since the **sign** value of drinking from the **chalice** in obedience to the **Lord's** command has been eliminated.

Introductory Dialogue   The first six lines of the **Eucharistic Prayer** spoken in dialogue between the **celebrant** and the **people**. "V. The **Lord** be with you. R. And with your spirit. V. Lift up your hearts. R. We lift them up to the Lord. V. Let us give thanks to the Lord our God. R. It is right and just." It is a very ancient part of the Eucharistic Prayer and may reach back to Apostolic times.

Introductory Rites   The beginning of **Mass** or another **liturgy**. The Introductory Rites at Mass usually consist of the **entrance procession**, the **Sign of the Cross**, the **greeting**, the **penitential act** or **rite of sprinkling**, the **Glory to God in the Highest** when prescribed, and the **collect**.

Introit   The **entrance antiphon**. In the Tridentine Missal the complete introit consisted of the **antiphon**, a **psalm** verse, the Glory to the Father, and a repetition of the antiphon.

Invitatory   (1) The introductory rite that begins the daily celebration of the **Liturgy of the Hours**. It consists of a short verse and response, "V. **Lord**, open my lips. R. And my mouth will **proclaim** your praise," followed by Psalm 95 with an **antiphon**. It precedes **Morning Prayer** or the **Office of Readings**, depending on which of these **offices** is prayed to begin the day.

(2) An invitation or other introduction directed to the **assembly** at **Mass** or another **liturgy**. In a general sense, any introduction to a prayer or **blessing** may be called an **invitatory**.

Invocation   A prayer or **petition** to God or to the **saints**, asking for help.

Invocative Form   The textual form in which God is invoked over the people, but in which the people are addressed directly. In other words, in these formulas, "you" means the people, rather than God. This is the characteristic form for the **blessings** at **Mass**—e.g., "May almighty God bless you." Alternative forms for such liturgical texts are called **deprecative** or **indicative**.

J

Jansenism   Rigorous teaching that the human being was basically depraved in nature, associated with Cornelius Jansen (1585–1638) and later condemned by the **Church**. His doctrines influenced Catholic piety to the extent that many people became overly scrupulous and absented themselves from communion, even at **Easter**.

John XXIII, Pope (1881–1963)   Born Angelo Roncalli, elected pope in 1958. He convened the Second Vatican Council, but died after the first session, before the Council issued its first document, the *Constitution on the Sacred Liturgy*. He is considered the originator of the movement towards *aggiornamento* (Italian, "updating") in the Catholic **Church** in the twentieth century. He was canonized in 2014.

John Chrysostom (347–407)   Patriarch of Constantinople and, along with **Basil**, Gregory the Theologian (Nazianzen), and Athanasius, one of the four great Greek **Doctors** of the **Church**. Many of his **sermons** are preserved, some of which give us an insight into the liturgical theology of his day. He is quoted as supporting the position that the words of **Christ** in the **Eucharistic Prayer** transform the **elements**.

Jungmann, Josef Andreas (1889–1975)   Austrian Jesuit liturgist. Among other works, he authored *The Mass of the Roman Rite*, one of the first detailed, historical analyses of the structure and origins of the **rituals** in the **Mass**. He also contributed to the revision of the Mass following the Second Vatican Council, serving as a consultor to the **Consilium**.

Justin (ca. 100–ca. 165)   Roman **martyr**, born in Syria, converted to Christianity around 130. His *Dialogue with Trypho* and his *First Apology* give us the earliest description of a Eucharistic celebration. After describing the sharing of Scriptures and the teaching of the presider, Justin turns to the Eucharist. He speaks of the blessed food as the **Eucharist**, declaring that they are not ordinary **bread** and **wine**, but the "flesh and blood of that **incarnate** Jesus." He mentions the prayer of praise and glory offered to God by the "**presider**" after which "all the people present give their assent by saying: **Amen.**"

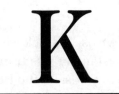

K

Kenosis The self-emptying of Jesus in becoming a member of the human race (cf. Philippians 2:7). This self-emptying is remembered in the **liturgy** as the **assembly celebrates** its union with **Christ** and its willingness to give of itself for the sake of others.

Kiss The form of reverence given the **altar** (after an initial **bow**) by **deacons**, **priests**, and **bishops** upon arriving in the **sanctuary** at the end of the **entrance procession**. At the end of **Mass**, the presiding priest and the deacon kiss the altar. The **Gospel** text is also kissed after its proclamation. At the **Celebration of the Lord's Passion** on **Good Friday**, the cross may be kissed during its veneration.

Kiss of Peace Another term for the **sign of peace**. The term originated in the ancient **Church**, where a kiss was exchanged as the sign of sharing the peace of **Christ**.

Kneeler A portable stand with a step, usually padded, at which one can kneel and, if needed, place a book for prayer or reading. It is also called a **prie-dieu**.

Kneeling The posture in which the body is supported by both knees on the ground or on a **kneeler**. It is a common posture for private prayer in the Western **Church** and can reflect a spirit of humility, repentance, or adoration.

Koinonia The Greek word for "communion." It is particularly used in reference to a unity between individuals fostered and **celebrated** in common **worship**. Acts 2:42 describes that the early Christians devoted themselves to "*koinonia*, the **breaking of the bread**, and prayer."

Kyrie   Vocative case of *kyrios*, a Greek word meaning "**lord**" or "master." When the Old Testament was translated into Greek, *kyrios* was the word used to translate the Hebrew words *Adonai* (my lord) or *YHWH* (I am who am), the name used for God in Exodus 3:14. In Philippians 2:11, Paul quotes a **hymn** that **proclaims**: "Jesus **Christ** is *Kyrios* to the glory of God the Father." In the **liturgy**, "**Kyrie, eleison**" originally was the response to a **litany** similar to the present **Universal Prayer**. It now forms a short litany addressed to Christ that is part of the **Introductory Rites** of the Mass.

Kyrie, Eleison   Greek for "**Lord**, have mercy." It is an **invocation** used in **litanies**, particularly in the **Introductory Rites**, sung alternately with "**Christe, eleison**" ("**Christ**, have mercy").

Laetare Sunday   Name given to the Fourth Sunday of **Lent**, taken from the first word of the **entrance antiphon** in **Latin**, "Rejoice, Jerusalem." **Rose**-colored vestments may be worn on this day instead of **violet**, and flowers may be used to decorate the **sanctuary**.

Lamb of God   The English name for the **Latin Agnus Dei**, a **litany** sung during the **breaking of the bread** during the **Fraction Rite** at **Mass**. The term is sometimes imprecisely used to refer to the Fraction Rite itself.

Lappets   The two strips of cloth, approximately two inches wide and eight inches long, that hang from the back of a **miter**.

Last Supper   The meal Jesus shared with his **Apostles** on the night before he died. The **Gospels** of Matthew, Mark, and Luke (the synoptic Gospels) describe it as a **Passover** meal, but John suggests that it was **celebrated** on the night before Passover began. The synoptic Gospels and St. Paul in 1 Corinthians 11:23–26 focus on the **institution** of the **Eucharist**, while the Gospel of John emphasizes the **Washing of Feet**.

Latin   The language traditionally used in **worship** by the **Roman Rite** of the Catholic **Church**. Liturgical books are first issued in Latin (**typical editions**) and then translated into other languages.

Latria   Adoration properly due to God alone or to one of the persons of the Trinity. It is distinguished from **dulia** and **hyperdulia**, which are the honor and praise given to the **saints** and to the Blessed Virgin Mary, respectively.

Lauds   The name often used for **Morning Prayer**, from the **Latin** for "praise."

Lavabo   A name sometimes used to refer to the **washing of hands** at **Mass**. It is derived from Psalm 26:6—"Lavabo inter innocentes manus meas: et circumdabo altare tuum, Domine" ("I will wash my hands in innocence that I may process around your **altar**, **Lord**"). In the Tridentine Missal this psalm was to be said quietly by the **priest** during the washing. The revised **Missal** uses a different text, taken from Psalm 51, but the older name for this action continues to be used.

Lavabo Bowl   The bowl used at the **washing of hands** at **Mass**.

Lay Faithful   All the baptized except those who are ordained.

Lay Minister   A member of the **lay faithful** who performs a designated liturgical action at **Mass** or other **liturgy**.

Laying on of Hands   A gesture of **blessing** or invocation mentioned in the New Testament in conjunction with prayer (e.g., Acts 13:3; 2 Timothy 1:6). The gesture is performed by extending both hands forward with the palms turned downward. Depending on the circumstances, the hands may be placed on the person's head or stretched out over a group of people or over an object. The gesture is used in many of the **sacraments** to indicate the conferral of special grace or the **invocation** of the Holy Spirit, as at **Ordination** and **Confirmation**, during **absolution** in the Sacrament of **Penance**, and at the invocation of the Spirit during a **Eucharistic Prayer**. The same gesture is also used during a solemn blessing or **prayer over the people** at the conclusion of Mass.

Lectern   A reading stand. Sometimes the **ambo** is referred to as the lectern. The ambo is reserved for the proclamation of **Sacred Scripture**, including the **responsorial psalm**; the **preaching** of the **homily**; the announcement of the intentions of the **Universal Prayer**; and the proclamation of the **Exsultet** at the **Easter Vigil**. A separate

lectern should be used for all other activities, such as leading song or making announcements. When both an ambo and a lectern are in the **sanctuary**, there should be a clear distinction between the two, with the ambo being more prominent and adorned.

Lectio Continua The continuous reading of Scripture at **Mass** and in the **Office of Readings** in the **Liturgy of the Hours**. It is an ancient tradition to read from Scripture in a continuous or semicontinuous manner, beginning one day where the previous day's reading ended. This tradition is followed for the most part in the **Sunday** and weekday **lectionary** cycles.

Lectionary for Mass The book containing the Scripture readings **proclaimed** at **Mass**, including the **responsorial psalms**, for each day of the year. The lectionary approved for use in the United States is published in several volumes. The **Gospel** readings are also contained in a separate *Book of the Gospels*.

Lector The liturgical **minister** who **proclaims** the biblical readings (except the Gospel) at liturgies. Although the title is frequently applied to any **reader**, *lector* more specifically refers to one who has been **instituted** in this ministry through the **Institution** of **Lectors**, which is **celebrated** almost exclusively for men preparing for **ordination**. Such ministers are called *instituted lectors*.

Lent The period that precedes the celebration of **Christ**'s Passion and Resurrection during the **Paschal Triduum**. Lent is both a time of preparation for **Baptism** and a penitential time; it is approximately forty days long, echoing the forty days of prayer and **fasting** of Jesus in the desert after his baptism. In the Western **Church**, it begins on **Ash Wednesday** and continues for six weeks. In the **Byzantine Rite**, it begins two days earlier, on the Monday prior to the First **Sunday** of Lent. It ends prior to the **Evening Mass of the Lord's Supper** on Holy Thursday. The last week of Lent is called **Holy Week**. For the **elect**, Lent is the **Period of Purification and Enlightenment**, the final preparation for **Baptism** at **Easter**. For the baptized, Lent is a **time** for renewal in the meaning and grace of their own Baptism. The **Alleluia** is not sung or said from the beginning of Lent until the **Easter Vigil**.

Lex Orandi, Lex Credendi   A standard maxim, frequently translated "the law of prayer is the law of belief," and attributed to Prosper of Aquitaine. The saying expresses the close interconnection between **worship** and faith; i.e., that which is expressed in prayer, especially in **liturgy**, is what the **Church** believes. Hence, liturgy is seen as "primary theology." Since liturgy is so crucial to forming believers in the Christian way of life, some contemporary authors have suggested that this maxim should be expanded to *lex orandi, lex credendi, lex vivendi*, "the law of prayer is the law of belief is the law of living."

Lights   A word that can be used for **candles** in **liturgy**.

Litany   A form of prayer in which a standard response is given to a series of **invocations**. In the Mass, the **Universal Prayer** and the **Agnus Dei** are both in the form of litanies. The **Kyrie** seems to be the response to a litany that disappeared somewhere in history. At **ordinations**, **religious professions**, and **baptisms**, the **Litany of the Saints** is prayed.

Litany of Supplication   Liturgical title used for the **Litany of the Saints** in the **Rites of Ordination of a Bishop, of Priests, and of Deacons**, part of the ***Roman Pontifical***.

Litany of the Saints   A **litany** that calls upon the **saints** to pray for the **Church**, believed to be the most ancient litany in the Church's **worship**. It is known to have been used as early as the year 590 by Pope **Gregory the Great** for a public **procession** of **thanksgiving**. It is used in various forms during the **Easter Vigil** for the **blessing** of the **baptismal font**, during the **Rite of Baptism**

for **Children**, during the **dedication of a church**, at **ordinations,** and as an option in the prayers for the **commendation of the dying**.

Liturgiam Authenticam   Document issued in 2001 by the **Congregation for Divine Worship and the Discipline of the Sacraments** on the use of **vernacular** languages in the publication of the books on the Roman **liturgy**. It is the fifth instruction guiding the implementation of the *Constitution on the Sacred Liturgy* of the Second Vatican Council. It is perhaps best noted for endorsing the principle of formal equivalence, a method of translation that is concerned with a precise fidelity to the sentence structure, style, and vocabulary of the original language.

Liturgical Calendar   A listing of dates of the year with the corresponding liturgical celebrations held on those dates. The General Roman Calendar, the basic calendar for the Roman Catholic **Church**, is found in the front of *The Roman Missal*. Nations, regions, dioceses, and religious institutes may have their own particular calendars, which supplement the general calendar.

Liturgical Reform Movement   The movement whose goal is the authentic **celebration** of the **liturgy** and the proper integration of liturgy within Christian life. The modern liturgical reform movement began in France in 1832 with the refounding of the Benedictine abbey of **Solesmes** by Dom **Prosper Guéranger**, and received a fresh start in 1909 with an address given at the National Congress of Catholic Works in Malines, Belgium, by Dom **Lambert Beauduin**. The goals of the movement were enshrined in *Sacrosanctum Concilium*, the Second Vatican Council's *Constitution on the Sacred Liturgy*, and the movement continues into the present as the reforms of the Council continue to be enacted and refined.

Liturgical Music Today   A 1982 statement of the United States National Conference of Catholic **Bishops** updating the earlier statement *Music in Catholic Worship*. Both statements have since been replaced by *Sing to the Lord: Music in Divine Worship*.

Liturgical Year   The annual cycle of liturgical celebrations, centered on the celebration of **Easter**. The liturgical year of the **Roman Rite** begins with the First **Sunday** of **Advent**. It comprises **Advent**, the four-week **time** of preparation for the Nativity of the **Lord; Christmas Time**, which extends from the Nativity of the Lord through the **Baptism of the Lord; Lent**, the six-week time of preparation for the **Paschal Triduum; Easter Time**, a fifty-day celebration of the Resurrection which concludes with Pentecost; and **Ordinary Time**. Ordinary Time is divided into two segments; the first occurs between the end of Christmas Time and the beginning of Lent, and the second from Pentecost to the beginning of Advent. The feast days of the Lord and of the **saints** add additional variety and richness to the **Church's** liturgical year.

Liturgy   Any official form of public **worship**, from the Greek word *leitourgia*, "work of the people." In the Eastern **churches**, the **Mass** is often called the Divine **Liturgy**. The title is frequently used in conjunction with a modifier, such as the **Liturgy of the Hours** or the **Liturgy of the Eucharist**. "The liturgy" is often used to refer to the Mass.

Liturgy Committee   A body of people charged with assisting the pastor, the **liturgy** director, other pastoral leadership, and the **assembly** in preparing for and enacting liturgical celebrations. Liturgy committees' structures and tasks vary greatly from parish to parish and diocese to diocese. They may be an advisory group to the pastor or liturgy director, or a committee of the parish pastoral council. The tasks of these committees may include long-range planning as well as specific tasks such as selecting music, preparing the environment, choosing certain options in the **rites**, and seeing to other practical details. Members of any liturgy committee should be properly formed to understand the **Church's** tradition and what is proper in the celebration of the sacred Liturgy.

Liturgy of the Eucharist   One of two major sections of the **Mass**, along with the **Liturgy of the Word**. It begins after the **Universal Prayer** and ends with the **prayer after communion**. It is structured around the **fourfold Eucharistic actions** of "take, bless, break, give," enacted in the presentation and **preparation of the gifts**, the **Eucharistic Prayer**, the **Fraction Rite**, and the **Communion Rite**.

Liturgy of the Hours   The official daily prayer of the **Church**, also called the **Divine Office** or the **breviary**. It is made up of the **canonical hours** of **Morning Prayer**, **Midday Prayer** (which consists of **Midmorning Prayer**, **Midday Prayer**, or **Midafternoon Prayer**), **Evening Prayer**, **Night Prayer**, and the **Office of Readings**. The hours are made up of hymns, **psalms, canticles**, Scripture readings, **intercessions**, and prayers. The Liturgy of the Hours is the daily prayer of the entire Church; all members are encouraged to pray some or all the hours, ideally in common in their parishes or other communities. Most clerics and vowed religious are canonically obligated to pray the Liturgy of the Hours.

Historically, two forms of the Liturgy of the Hours developed in the early Church in response to different contexts. The **cathedral** form was **celebrated** by the whole Christian community and was originally presided over by the **bishop**; it consisted of prayer in the morning and evening. Morning Prayer was related to praise for creation and the Resurrection, and Evening Prayer was related to **petition** and **intercession** for salvation. A limited number of the **psalms**, **hymns**, Scripture readings, and prayers were used over a period of time. The monastic form centered on the praying of all the **psalms** over a given period of time and a larger selection of Scripture. It was appropriate for a stable community, as found in a monastery. From this form the night office and the various **midday prayers** developed.

Liturgy of the Word One of two major sections of the **Mass**, along with the **Liturgy of the Eucharist**. It follows the **Introductory Rites** and ends with the **Universal Prayer**. On **Sundays** and solemnities, it consists of the **first reading**, usually from the Old Testament; the **responsorial psalm**; the **second reading**, from one of the New Testament letters or Revelation; the **Alleluia** or **verse before the Gospel**; the Gospel; a **homily**; the **Profession of Faith** and the **Universal Prayer**. On weekdays, only one reading precedes the Gospel and the Profession of Faith is not prescribed.

Lord A biblical and liturgical title now used for any person of the Trinity. In the **Glory to God in the Highest**, God the Father is addressed as "Lord God, heavenly King," and Jesus is addressed as "Lord Jesus **Christ**." In the **Niceno-Constantinopolitan Creed**, the Holy Spirit is said to be the "Lord and giver of life." *Lord* is used to translate the Hebrew name of God, written as YHWH in the Old Testament and spoken as *Adonai*, and the Greek *Kyrios* or *Kyrie*. That title for God was transferred to Jesus in the Christian era and has been used in the **liturgy** from early days.

Lord's Day Another name for **Sunday**. It was used as early as the first century, in the *Didache*.

Lord's Prayer The prayer taught by Jesus to his **disciples**. Although two forms appear in the **Gospels**, a longer form in Matthew 6:9–13 and a shorter form in Luke 11:2–4, the **Church** has regularly used an adaptation of the form in the Gospel of Matthew, which also appears in the *Didache* (chapter 8), with minor changes. The final **doxology** of the prayer ("For the kingdom, the power, and the glory are yours now and for ever.") appears in the *Didache* and some manuscripts of Matthew; it used in the **Roman Rite** and the **Byzantine Rite**. In the Roman Rite, an **embolism** is prayed by the **priest** before the doxology.

Lord's Supper   A name taken from 1 Corinthians 11:20, sometimes used for the **Mass**, to emphasize its connection to the **Last Supper**. The term is used on the evening of the **Thursday of the Lord's Supper**, when the principal **liturgy** is called the **Evening Mass of the Lord's Supper**.

Lord's Table   A term sometimes used to refer to the **altar**.

Low Church   A term sometimes used to describe those communities who practice a style of **liturgy** that emphasizes the word and **preaching**, and uses a minimum of **ritual** or sacramental **rites**. A contrasting term is "**high church**."

Low Sunday   The name formerly given in English to the **Sunday** after **Easter**, because of the contrast to the Easter celebration on the previous weekend. In **Latin**, the title was *Dominica in albis* ("Sunday in **white**") referring to the **white garments** that the newly baptized wore until this day.

Lucernarium   A **blessing** or lighting of lamps at evening, giving thanks to God for the day, usually taking place as the start of an evening **service**. The lucernarium was derived from the Hebrew blessing of the evening lamp and has a very ancient tradition in the Christian **church**. The **Easter Vigil** begins with a lucernarium, and some communities occasionally add a lucernarium before **Evening Prayer** on special celebrations.

Lunette   The container with glass sides that holds a large **host** and is placed in a **monstrance** for **exposition of the Blessed Sacrament**.

M

Magisterium   The teaching authority of the **Church** conferred upon the **Apostles** by **Christ** and now residing in their successors, the **bishops**, in union with the pope, the successor of St. Peter.

Magnificat   The **Canticle of Mary**.

Mandatum   **Latin** for "commandment," the first word of John 13:34 in Latin, "Mandatum novum do vobis" ("I give you a new commandment"). It is often used to refer to the **rite** of **Washing of Feet** on **Holy Thursday**.

Marialis Cultus   The apostolic exhortation of **Pope Paul VI** issued in 1974 concerning devotion to the Blessed Virgin Mary. It is considered to be one of the most important **Church** documents on **Marian devotion**.

Maria Laach   A Benedictine monastery in Rhineland, Germany, home of Dom **Odo Casel**. With **Solesmes**, it was one of the centers for liturgical renewal in the late nineteenth and early twentieth centuries, the beginnings of the **liturgical movement**.

Marian Devotions   Devotions to the Blessed Virgin Mary, the mother of Jesus. These include public recitation of prayers like the **Rosary**, the **Litany** of Loreto, and the Angelus, special **rites** like the Crowning of an Image of the Blessed Virgin Mary, and **processions**.

Marriage   The permanent union of man and woman in a covenant of love. The marriage of two baptized Christians is considered a sacrament—i.e., the Sacrament of **Matrimony**.

Matrimony   The **sacrament** by which a baptized man and baptized woman, by expressing their **consent**, enter into a permanent union in a covenant of love. Natural **marriage** comes from God and is divinely blessed, but the marriage of two baptized Christians is considered a sacrament. Through Matrimony, married Christians signify and share in the **mystery** of the unity and fruitful love that exists between **Christ** and his **Church**.

Martyr   Someone who is killed because of his or her allegiance to **Christ**. Some **saints** who died violent deaths may not be considered martyrs if their deaths were due to nonreligious issues. Joan of Arc is one such saint.

Mass   The name for the entire celebration of the **Eucharist** of the **Roman Rite**. It is derived from the **Latin** word for "**dismissal**," *missa*.

Mass of Christian Burial   Term sometimes used for the **Funeral Mass**.

Mass of the Resurrection   A term sometimes used incorrectly to refer to the **Funeral Mass**. This title is properly given only to Masses **celebrated** on **Easter**.

Mass Offering   A monetary donation given to a **priest** with the understanding that **Mass** will be **celebrated**. Often called a *stipend*, the word used in the 1917 *Code of Canon Law*, the 1983 *Code of Canon Law* calls it an offering. According to canon 946, Mass **offerings** are a contribution "to the good of the **church** . . . to support its **ministers** and works." A priest may keep one such offering per day.

Mass for the Dead   A category of **Masses** in *The Roman Missal* to pray specifically for the deceased, expressing that all the members of the body of **Christ**, whether living or deceased, are in union with one another and thus bringing comfort to those who are mourning. The **Funeral Mass** is the primary celebration in this category, which also includes commemorations on the anniversaries of death and other occasions.

Mass for the People   The **Mass** said by **bishops** of dioceses and by pastors of parishes for the people entrusted to their care. A Mass for the People is required to be **celebrated** each **Sunday** and **holyday of obligation**.

Mass of the Lord's Supper   The **Mass celebrated** on the evening of **Thursday of the Lord's Supper**. This first **liturgy** of the **Paschal Triduum** commemorates the **institution** of the Eucharist and of thepriesthood, and the giving of the commandment of the Lord concerning charity toward one another. At this Mass, the **Washing of Feet** may take place after the **homily**, and at the very end of the Mass there is a **procession** with the **bread consecrated** for the **Celebration of the Passion of the Lord** the next day.

Masses for Various Needs and Occasions   A category of Masses in *The Roman Missal* that covers a variety of needs of the **Church** and the world. These Mass formularies include Masses for vocations, for the family, for the unity of Christians; Masses for civil needs, for those in public **office**, in time of war or civil disturbance, after the harvest; and for various other intentions such as for the forgiveness of sins, charity, or the sick.

Master of Ceremonies   The liturgical **minister** who directs the presiding **priest** and other ministers, particularly at more solemn **services**, and ensures that the **liturgy** is carried out properly and with due reverence.

Matter   The physical material and the gestures that together form the major visible aspect of a **sacrament**. Matter is frequently linked to **form** (the formula or words used) in describing a sacramental **rite**. The matter of the **Eucharist** has traditionally been seen as the wheat **bread** and grape **wine**, and the matter of **Baptism** has been the washing with **water** by pouring or **immersion**.

Maundy Thursday   An old English name for **Holy Thursday**, derived from the **Latin** title for the **rite** of **Washing of Feet**, the **Mandatum**.

McManus, Frederick (1923–2005)   American liturgist and canonist. Former Dean of the School of **Canon** Law at the Catholic University of America and former director of the US **Bishops'** Committee on the **Liturgy**, he was one of the few Americans who served as a consultor to the postconciliar commission (the **Consilium**) that revised the **Mass** in the years following the Second Vatican Council. McManus was also noted for his key role in bringing the liturgy into the **vernacular**.

Mediator Dei   The encyclical of Pope Pius XII promulgated in 1947 that gave official support and encouragement to the **liturgical reform movement**.

Memorial   (1) A common way of translating the word **anamnesis** and of understanding the concept. In liturgical theology, however, anamnesis is not understood as a memorial ceremony that merely recalls a past event. It is understood, rather, as the active remembrance and making present of a saving reality.

(2) The rank of liturgical days lower than both **solemnities** and **feasts**. Memorials may be classified as either **obligatory** or **optional**. On the weekdays of **Lent**, the weekdays of **Advent** from December 17 to 24, and the days within the **Octave** of Christmas, all memorials are considered optional and may be observed only as **commemorations**.

Memorial Acclamation   The **acclamation** made by the **assembly** during the **Eucharistic Prayer**, after the **Institution Narrative** and the invitation, "The **mystery** of faith." Three possible texts are given in *The Roman Missal*. Each acclamation refers in some way to the **Paschal Mystery** and the second coming of **Christ**.

Mensa   The top of the **altar**. According to the *General Instruction of the Roman Missal*, the mensa should be made of natural stone; in the dioceses of the United States, it may be made of solid and dignified wood.

Midafternoon Prayer   One of the hours of **Daytime Prayer** in the **Liturgy of the Hours**, said in the middle of the afternoon, between **Midday Prayer** and **Evening Prayer**.

Midday Prayer   One of the hours of **Daytime Prayer** in the **Liturgy of the Hours**, said in the middle of the day, between **Midmorning Prayer** and **Midafternoon Prayer**, around noontime.

Midmorning Prayer   One of the hours of **Daytime Prayer** in the **Liturgy of the Hours**, said in the middle of the morning, between **Morning Prayer** and **Midday Prayer**.

Michel, Virgil (1888–1938)   Benedictine monk of St. John's Abbey in Collegeville, Minnesota. He was founder and first editor of the journal *Worship*, originally titled ***Orate Fratres***. This work gave rise to the establishment of the Liturgical Press. A tireless worker, he believed that good **liturgy** was not the preserve of monasteries, and he campaigned to unite liturgy and life, **ritual** and social justice.

Minister   Anyone who serves the worshipping community by performing some function in the **liturgy** or assisting others in performing theirs. The ordained clergy are referred to as "sacred ministers" in order to distinguish them from the nonordained ministers in a liturgy. Some of the more common liturgical ministers are **reader** or **lector, acolyte, altar server, usher, choir, cantor,** 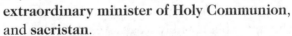 **extraordinary minister of Holy Communion,** and **sacristan**.

Minister of Hospitality   An alternative name for a **greeter** or an **usher**, particularly if the primary task is that of welcoming people at the doors of the **church** or showing hospitality in other ways before or after the **liturgy**.

Ministerial Priesthood   The ordained priesthood, distinct from the **priesthood of the faithful**. The term designates the status of one ordained to the **order** of **presbyter** by the **Sacrament** of **Holy Orders**, sharing in the priesthood of **Christ** and empowered to offer the **sacrifice** of the **Mass**.

Minor Exorcisms   Rites belonging to the period of the catechumenate in the *Rite of Christian Initiation of Adults*. They are meant to highlight the struggle with evil in the Christian life, the importance of self-denial, and the constant need for God's help. A **priest**, **deacon**, or a catechist appointed by the **bishop** may be the **celebrant** for these **rituals**, which may be held at the beginning or end of a meeting for catechesis, or even **celebrated** privately for an individual **catechumen**.

Missa pro Populo   Latin for "Mass for the People."

Missal   A **ritual** book containing all the texts, readings, and prayers needed for the celebration of the **Mass**. The term is often used as a reference to the current *Roman Missal*.

Miter   The hat used by a **bishop** as a **sign** of his **office**. In the West, the miter is pointed, has two **lappets**, and is made so that when not worn it lies flat. In the **Byzantine Rite**, the miter is shaped like an imperial crown. The miter may also be worn by certain **priests** as a sign of their **office**—e.g., abbots. In the West, those who wear a miter also wear a **zucchetto** under it. The miter need not be worn at every Mass, but it is normally worn at more solemn liturgies.

Miter Bearer   The name given to the **minister** who holds the **bishop's miter** when it is not being worn. This minister may also bring the miter to and take the miter from the bishop as needed. The miter bearer may wear a **vestment** known as a **vimpa** while performing this ministry.

Mixed Chalice   The cup containing both **water** and **wine**. Several ancient liturgical texts refer to a "mixed chalice" rather than merely a cup of wine. The mixture is a **symbol** of **Christ** who in his person unites the divine (symbolized by wine) with the human (symbolized by water).

Monstrance   The vessel used to display a large **consecrated host** during **exposition of the Blessed Sacrament**. While there are many different designs and styles for monstrances, it always has a base so that it can stand upright on a flat surface, e.g., the **altar**, and a clear round window where the **lunette** with the host is placed.

Morning Prayer   One of the **canonical hours** of the **Liturgy of the Hours**, sometimes referred to by its older name of **Lauds**. Celebrated in the light of a new day, Morning Prayer recalls the Resurrection of the **Lord** Jesus, the true light who enlightens all. In the present **Roman Rite**, it consists of the introductory verse, a **hymn**, **psalmody** (two **psalms** and a **canticle**), a reading from Scripture with its **responsory**, the **Canticle of Zechariah**, **intercessions**, the Our Father, and a concluding prayer and **blessing**. Along with **Evening Prayer**, it is one of the primary hours of the Liturgy of the Hours.

Morse   The ornate clasp on a **cope**, also called a fibula.

Motu Proprio   **Latin** for "of his own accord." A term used of certain papal documents, signifying that the content of the document and its promulgation were decided on by the pope himself.

Movable Altar   An **altar** that is not attached to the floor. A movable altar should be dedicated according to the proper **ritual**, although it is permissible for it simply to be **blessed**.

Music in Catholic Worship   The 1972 statement, revised in 1983, of the US National Conference of Catholic **Bishops** regarding the use of music in the **liturgy**. It expanded on suggestions found in the then-current edition of the *General Instruction of the Roman Missal* and elsewhere, and gave additional guidelines based on the literary characteristics of the English language. A supplementary statement, *Liturgical Music Today*, was issued on the tenth anniversary of the original statement. Both documents have since been replaced by *Sing to the Lord: Music in Divine Worship*.

Mustum   Fresh grape juice that has just begun the fermentation process. Permission for the use of mustum in place of **wine** at **Mass** may be obtained for special situations, such as when a **priest** suffers from severe allergies or from alcoholism.

Mystagogical Catechesis   The postbaptismal instruction given to the newly baptized, or **neophytes**, especially during **Easter Time**. The name is first found in the writings of **Cyril of Jerusalem**.

Mystagogy   Postbaptismal instruction, also called **mystagogical catechesis**. It is also the name of the final stage or period in the process of the *Rite of Christian Initiation of Adults*, a time for the newly initiated, along with the whole community, to begin to understand more deeply the meaning of the mysteries they have received and to become more deeply immersed in the life of the **Church**. The *Rite of Christian Initiation of Adults* suggests that the **bishop** meet with the newly initiated during the period of mystagogy and preside at a celebration of the **Eucharist** with them. The period usually closes with **Pentecost** at the conclusion of **Easter Time**, when a special celebration is recommended. The *National Statutes for the Catechumenate*, 24, direct that after the immediate mystagogy of **Easter Time**, the postbaptismal ministry to the neophytes should last at least one year.

Mystery   In Christian usage, something that has such depth and richness of meaning that, while it can be experienced, it can never be fully comprehended or explained. St. Paul speaks about the **Gospel** revealing the mystery hidden for all ages (Romans 16:25), and thus the term is connected with the unfolding of the plan of God for salvation as it is revealed to human beings. Especially in Greek writings, the **sacraments** are called mysteries.

N

Narthex   The space inside the entrance of a **church** where people may gather before or after **liturgy**. It can be a place of welcome, a transitional space from the outside world into the **worship** space of the church, and vice versa. Some liturgical moments may occur in the narthex, such as the **introductory rites** of the **Rite** of Acceptance into the **Order of Catechumens**, of the **Rite of Baptism for Children**, and of the **Funeral Liturgy**.

National Statutes for the Catechumenate   A document, issued by the United States **bishops** in 1986 and confirmed by the Apostolic See in 1988, that governs the **catechumenate** in the United States.

Nave   The main section of a **church** building where the **assembly** gathers for **worship**. It is the area in the church building for the faithful containing the **pews**, distinct from the **sanctuary**.

Neophyte   A newly baptized Christian.

Niceno-Constantinopolitan Creed   The standard form of the **Profession of Faith** used at Mass; also called the Nicene **Creed**. It was first approved at the First Council of Nicaea in 325 and again at the Council of Constantinople in the somewhat modified form that is now used. It is professed by all Catholic and Orthodox **churches** and in most Protestant denominations.

Night Prayer   The last **office** of the **Liturgy of the Hours**, sometimes called **Compline**. It consists of an introductory verse, an **examination of conscience**, a **hymn**, **psalmody**, a scriptural reading with its **responsory**, the **Canticle of Simeon**, a concluding prayer, a **blessing**, and an **antiphon** in honor of the Blessed Virgin Mary.

Norms for the Distribution and Reception of Holy Communion under Both Kinds in the Dioceses of the United States of America Document issued by the **United States Conference of Catholic Bishops** and confirmed by the Apostolic See that gives norms for the administration of **communion under both kinds**. It went into effect in 2002 and has the force of particular law for the Roman Catholic dioceses of the United States.

Novena A devotion that is **celebrated** for nine days, which sometimes precedes an important liturgical day. It usually consists of special prayers and public liturgies.

Nunc Dimittis The **Canticle of Simeon**.

Nuptial Blessing The **blessing** imparted to a newly married couple at the celebration of the **Sacrament** of **Matrimony**. In the **Order** of Celebrating **Matrimony** within **Mass**, the Nuptial Blessing is given in place of the **embolism** and **doxology** of the **Lord's Prayer**. In the Order of Celebrating Matrimony without Mass, the Nuptial Blessing is given after the last **intercession** in the **Universal Prayer**.

Nuptial Mass Alternative term for the celebration of **Matrimony** within **Mass**.

O

Oblation   The act of offering. The term is also used for the **offerings** of **bread** and **wine** at **Mass**.

Obligatory Memorial   A liturgical day with the rank of **memorial**. On such a day, the **Mass** of the memorial is to be used, rather than the weekday Mass of the current liturgical **time**. Contrasts with **optional memorial**.

Octave   The eight-day period during which a liturgical commemoration is **celebrated**. It consists of the day itself and the seven days following. **Christmas** and **Easter** each have octaves. The term is also used informally to refer to the eighth day of the octave.

Offerings   (1) The **gifts** of **bread** and **wine**. They symbolize the offering of self that each member of the **assembly** makes as participation in **Christ's** offering of himself to God the Father. This participation in the offering is expressed in many of the **Prayers over the Offerings** and in the **anamnesis** section of the **Eucharistic Prayer** as varying words articulate the liturgical dynamic of "we remember, therefore we offer."
   (2) The term *offering* is sometimes used for the monetary donation given to a **priest** with the understanding that **Mass** will be celebrated. See **Mass offering**.

Offertory   Term from the Tridentine Missal that sometimes is still used to refer to what is now called the **preparation of the gifts**. Although the **bread** and **wine** are referred to as **offerings**, this part of the **Mass** involves their presentation and preparation for the act of offering, which takes place during the **Eucharistic Prayer**. Nevertheless, the **chant** that occurs at the preparation of the gifts is still referred to as the **offertory chant**.

Offertory Chant   The song that accompanies the **procession with the gifts** of **bread** and **wine** to the **altar** during **Mass**.

Offertory Procession   Another name used for the **procession with the gifts** of **bread** and **wine** to the **altar** during **Mass**—i.e., the presentation of the gifts.

Offertory Table   Another name for the **gift table**.

Office   (1) In general, any duty that one performs or assumes, especially one conferred by **ordination**.
(2) The **Liturgy of the Hours** in its entirety or one of those hours—e.g., office of **Morning Prayer**, office of **Night Prayer**.

Office for the Dead   A complete **office** in the **Liturgy of the Hours** with special texts for remembering the dead. It is used on **All Souls' Day** and at other times to pray for the dead, such as on the day of a death or funeral, or an anniversary of death.

Office of Readings   One of the hours of the **Liturgy of the Hours**. It is primarily a liturgical celebration of the **Word of God**. It may be prayed at any time of day, or in combination with another office, usually **Morning Prayer**.

Oil of Catechumens   One of the three **holy oils**. It is used to **anoint** catechumens during their time of formation and infants in the **Rite of Baptism for Children**. It is stored in a decanter or **oil stock** usually labeled OC.

Oil of the Sick   One of the three **holy oils**. It is used to **anoint** the sick, usually on the forehead and on the palms of the hands, in the celebration of the **Anointing of the Sick**. It is stored in a decanter or **oil stock** labeled OI, for *oleum infirmorum*, "oil of the sick."

Oil Stock   A small vial or vessel in which one of the **holy oils** is kept for immediate use by a **priest**. Large decanters or other vessels are appropriate for storage and/or display of the holy oils in the **ambry**.

Ombrellino   (1) A large umbrella with a bent stem, intended to be carried by a **minister** over a **priest** carrying the **Blessed Sacrament**.
   (2) The **red** and **gold** papal umbrella, or *conopaeum*, which, with the *tintinnabulum* (**bell** tree), is one of the privileges of a minor **basilica**.

Opening Prayer   The term used to refer to the **collect** of the **Mass** in the *Order of Christian Funerals* and in the previous English language version of *The Roman Missal* (called the **Sacramentary** in some countries).

Optional Memorial   A liturgical day with the rank of **memorial**. On such a day, the **Mass** of the memorial may be used but is not obligatory. Another Mass, even the weekday Mass of the current liturgical **time**, may be **celebrated**. Contrasts with **obligatory memorial**.

Orans Position   A posture of prayer in which the arms are uplifted toward heaven, stretched out slightly forward, with palms upward. Many old **icons** depict the **saints** in prayer with arms in this position. It is the position used by the presiding **priest** when saying the **presidential prayers** at **liturgy**—e.g., the **orations** at **Mass**.

Orate Fratres   (1) **Latin** for "Pray, brethren," a term that refers to the moment in the **Mass** just before the **prayer over the offerings** where the **priest** says, "Pray, brethren (brothers and sisters), that my **sacrifice** and yours may be acceptable to God, the almighty Father."
   (2) The original name for the liturgical journal now called *Worship*.

Oration   In general, any liturgical prayer. When used in the plural, the term usually refers to the three **presidential prayers** at Mass—i.e., the **collect**, the **prayer over the offerings**, and the **prayer after communion.**

Oratory   A place of prayer other than a parish church that has been set aside by the proper **Church** authority, in accord with canon 1223 of the 1983 *Code of Canon Law*, for **liturgy** and devotional **services.**

Order   (1) A group of persons having a common bond, similar identity, or standing in the **Church**—e.g, the **order of catechumens**, or living under common religious regulations as in an institute of consecrated life, such as the Order of Friars Minor (Franciscans), the Order of Preachers (Dominicans), or the Order of Discalced Carmelites (Carmelite nuns)

(2) A single level, or **choir,** in the **hierarchy** of **angels.**

(3) A prescribed form of a liturgical **ritual,** such as the *Order of Christian Funerals*, or the Order of **Mass.**

(4) One of the three levels of ordained ministry: the order of **deacons,** the order of the **presbyterate,** the order of **bishops.**

Order of Catechumens   The group to which an unbaptized **adult** who is preparing to receive the **sacraments of initiation** belongs after celebrating the **Rite** of Acceptance into the Order of **Catechumens.**

Order of Celebrating Matrimony   The **ritual** book, part of the *Roman Ritual*, that contains the **rites** for the celebration of the **Sacrament** of **Matrimony** and other celebrations related to **marriage.** This is the English translation of the second **typical edition**; it came into use in the United States in 2016.

Order of Christian Funerals   The **ritual** book, part of the ***Roman Ritual***, which contains all the funeral **rites** for the Roman Catholic Church. Included are rites for the moments immediately after death, for **gathering in the presence of the body,** for transferring the body to the church or to the place of committal; the **Vigil Service**; the **Funeral Liturgy**; and the **Rite of Committal.** The **Office for the Dead** is also included in the ritual book.

Ordinary   (1) Those texts in a **liturgy** that generally do not vary, although they may not always be used on every occasion. The Ordinary of the **Mass** includes the **Eucharistic Prayer**, for example, even though there are several Eucharistic Prayers which may be chosen, and also includes the **Glory to God in the Highest** and the **Profession of Faith**, even though these may not be said at every Mass. The ordinary of a liturgy is distinct from the **proper**, which refers to those texts that are particularly assigned to a given day or liturgical celebration.

(2) The term is also used to refer to the **diocesan bishop**, since he has ordinary jurisdiction in his diocese. It may also refer to some religious superiors in particular circumstances.

Ordinary Form of the Mass   The **Mass celebrated** according to the post–Vatican II **Order** of Mass promulgated in 1969 by **Pope Paul VI** and reissued in the third **typical edition** of *The Roman Missal* by Pope John Paul II in 2000. This Mass reflects the reform of the **liturgy** that was undertaken after the Second Vatican Council. The term distinguishes this form of the Mass from the **extraordinary form**.

Ordinary Minister   Those who have a particular duty in the Church as part of their **office** as **deacon**, **priest**, or **bishop**. For example, ordained ministers are ordinary ministers of **Holy Communion**; bishops are ordinary ministers of **Confirmation**.

Ordinary Time The liturgical **time** that does not **celebrate** any particular aspect of the **mystery** of **Christ**, but rather the mystery of Christ in its fullness. It spans two periods of the **liturgical calendar**. The first period begins on the day following the **Feast of the Baptism of the Lord** and continues through the Tuesday before **Ash Wednesday**; the second begins on the day after **Pentecost** and continues until **Evening Prayer** I of the First **Sunday** of **Advent**. The term *ordinary* refers to the term *ordinal*, as in numerical, referring to the numerical titles given to the Sundays of this period, such as the Third Sunday in **Ordinary Time**.

Ordination The act of conferring the **Sacrament** of Holy Orders. Common to the celebration the sacrament for the orders of **deacon**, **priest**, and **bishop** is the questioning of the candidates, the **Litany of Supplication** with the prostration of the **candidates**, the **laying on of hands**, and the Prayer of Ordination.

Ordo (1) A term used for the **order** or **ordinary** of the **Mass**, especially used of the Roman *ordines*, documents that described the early Roman liturgies.

(2) A term that can be used interchangeably with *rite* to designate groups of **rituals**, as in the title *Order of Christian Funerals*.

(3) The detailed annual **liturgical calendar** that indicates which liturgical celebrations occur on which days, and which texts can or must be used in the celebration of **Mass** and of the **Liturgy of the Hours** on a specific day.

Orthodoxy Derived from the Greek for "correct praise" (or "right worship"), and also meaning "correct belief." The title *Orthodox* is used by Eastern Christian Churches that have been in communion with the Patriarch of Constantinople since the Great Schism of 1054, and is frequently applied to the **Byzantine Rite** and its style of worship.

Orthopraxis   Derived from the Greek for "correct action" and frequently used in conjunction with **orthodoxy**. The implication is that correct **worship** of God leads to correct interaction with other people in the living out of the **Gospel**.

Ostensorium   Another name for the **monstrance**.

Otto, Rudolf (1869–1937)   Theologian who specialized in the history and phenomenology of religion. Author of *The Idea of the Holy*.

P

Pall   (1) The large **white** cloth used to cover the coffin of the deceased during the **funeral liturgy** as a reminder of the **baptismal** garment.

   (2) A flat, cloth-covered board, about six inches square, used to cover the **chalice** to keep insects out. Its use is optional.

Pallbearer   A person who, with several others, carries the coffin of the deceased into and out of **church** for the **funeral liturgy** and, often, to the place where the **Rite of Committal** will take place.

Pallium   A **vestment** worn by archbishops and the pope. It is a two-inch wide circular band made of white woolen cloth with six black **crosses** embroidered on it. It is worn encircling the neck, over the shoulders, outside the **chasuble**, with one band hanging down over the chest and one band hanging down over the back. When the Pope wears the pallium, it signifies the fullness of his **office**; when an archbishop wears it, it symbolizes his communion with papal authority and with the **Church**.

Palms   Branches waved during the **Lord's** entry into Jerusalem at **Passover** time before his Death. Palms or branches of other trees are blessed on **Palm Sunday of the Lord's Passion** as part of the extended **entrance procession**. Leftover palms are traditionally burned and the **ashes** used on **Ash Wednesday** the following year.

Palm Sunday of the Lord's Passion   The **Sunday** before **Easter**, the beginning of **Holy Week**. On this day, the entry of **Christ** into Jerusalem before his Death is commemorated. During **Masses** on this day, a special **procession** may commemorate the **Lord's** entrance into Jerusalem with a **rite** that includes the **blessing** of **palms** and a reading of a **Gospel** account of the Lord's entry into Jerusalem. After the procession, in which all or part of the **congregation** may join, Mass continues with the **collect**. During the **Liturgy of the Word** the Gospel is a reading of the **Passion** narrative from Matthew, Mark, or Luke.

Parsch, Pius (1884–1954) German liturgist and author of *The Church's Year of Grace*, among other important works. He is noted for his efforts in the popular catechesis on the **liturgy**.

Particular Church A term used in liturgical documents that means a diocese, that part of the **People of God** entrusted to the pastoral care of a **bishop**, assisted by his **priests**. Gathered together in the Holy Spirit through the **Gospel** and the **Eucharist**, the one, holy, catholic, and apostolic Church is truly present and at work in a particular **Church**.

Pascha The Greek word which translates the Hebrew word for **Passover**. It is also used for **Christ**'s own passing over from death to life (John 13:1), that is, the Resurrection, or **Easter**. Many Eastern Christians prefer the term *Pascha* to *Easter* when referring to Christ's Resurrection. *Pascha*, when referring to Christ and Christians, may mean "passage," recalling the passage through the Red Sea of the Hebrews fleeing slavery in Egypt and the passage of Christ through death to life. It may also mean **passion**, in the sense of suffering, especially of Christ himself.

Paschal Of or having to do with the **Pascha**. It is often used as an adjective designating a connection with **Easter**.

Paschal Candle The large **candle** that is inscribed, lighted, and carried in **procession** at the beginning of the **Easter Vigil**. During **Easter Time** it is given a prominent place near the **ambo** or in the middle of the **sanctuary** and is lit during **Masses** and other **services** throughout the fifty days of Easter Time. After **Pentecost**, it is kept in the **baptistery** and is lit during the celebration of **Baptism**. It is also lit at funerals, and may be placed at the head of the coffin. The **Paschal candle** must be a genuine candle made of wax, and renewed each year; there is to be only one Paschal candle in a **church**. It is also called the **Easter candle**.

Paschal Fast   The **fasting** associated with the **Paschal Triduum**, described in the *Constitution on the Sacred Liturgy*, 110. It begins after the **Evening Mass of the Lord's Supper** on **Holy Thursday** and continues on **Good Friday** and even on **Holy Saturday** until the **Easter Vigil**. This fast is undertaken not in a spirit of **penance** as in the **Lenten** fast, but rather in a spirit of preparation, excitement, and anticipation of Easter joy.

Paschal Mystery   The saving **mystery** of **Christ**'s Passion, Death, and Resurrection. It is the mystery that is **celebrated** and made present in every **liturgy**, and the mystery that every Christian is to imitate and be united with in everyday life. In general, then, it can also refer spiritually to any event in which the experience of joy arising through sorrow or new life coming out of death is achieved and experienced in union with Christ's own Death and Resurrection. While every liturgical celebration is founded on the Paschal Mystery, it is especially celebrated during the **Paschal Triduum**.

Paschal Time   Another name for **Easter Time**, or the **Easter Season**.

Paschal Triduum   The three-day celebration of the **Paschal Mystery** of **Christ** that is the high point and center of the entire **liturgical year**. The Paschal Triduum begins with the **Evening Mass of the Lord's Supper** on **Holy Thursday**, solemnly remembers Christ's Death on **Good Friday**, reaches its zenith with the **Easter Vigil** with the **Baptism** of the elect into the mystery of Christ's Death and Resurrection, and concludes with **Evening Prayer** of **Easter Sunday**. Although each day has a different emphasis, the texts of all the prayers mention the complete mystery of **Christ**'s Death and Resurrection.

Paschal Vigil   Another name for the **Easter Vigil**.

Passion of the Lord   The events of the suffering and Death of the Lord Jesus, as recounted in the four **Gospels**. The Passion of the Lord is **proclaimed** at **Mass** on **Palm Sunday of the Lord's Passion** (from Matthew, Mark, or Luke, depending on the **lectionary** cycle) and at the **Celebration of the Passion of the Lord** on **Good Friday** (from the Gospel of John). On both days the Passion is proclaimed without **candles** and without **incense**, and the **greeting** and the signing of the book are both omitted. The Passion may be **chanted** or proclaimed, with several different **priests,** deacons, or **readers** taking parts in the proclamation. Traditionally, one person takes the role of a narrator, another (a deacon or priest if possible) speaks the words of Christ, and a third person speaks the words of other individuals.

Passiontide   A name formerly used for the last two weeks of **Lent**. The Fifth **Sunday** of **Lent** was formerly called the First Sunday in Passiontide, and on that Sunday all **statues** and **crosses** in **churches** were covered with purple **veils**. These veils were removed during the **Glory to God in the Highest** at the **Easter Vigil**. The revised *Missal* allows the veiling but does not require it, and, if covered, crosses are uncovered at the end of the **Celebration of the Lord's Passion on Good Friday**, and images are uncovered for the beginning of the Easter Vigil.

Passover   The Jewish feast commemorating the Exodus of the Israelites from Egypt (Exodus 12). Jesus **celebrated** the **Last Supper** and died in the context of the Passover feast (cf. John 12:1) and his **Paschal Mystery** is sometimes called his Passover. In the First Letter to the Corinthians (5:7) Paul refers to **Christ** himself as our Passover. The word is translated into Greek as **Pascha**.

Pastoral Care of the Sick: Rites of Anointing and Viaticum   **Ritual** book that is part of the *Roman Ritual* and gives the rites for ministering to the sick and dying. Included are **rites** for visiting the sick, for bringing **Holy Communion** to the sick, for the **Sacrament** of the **Anointing of the Sick,** and for ministering to the dying and at the time of death. Many of the rites in this book may be led by **deacons** or even by laypersons in addition to **priests**.

Pastoral Staff   The large staff made of wood or metal carried by the **bishop** in **procession** and held by him at certain times in liturgies. In Western **churches** it is normally shaped like a shepherd's crook. In some Eastern churches, the top of the staff has two snakes intertwined and facing each other, symbolic of the staffs of Moses and Aaron which turned into snakes (Exodus 4:2–3, 7:9). In the **Roman Rite**, the bishop holds the staff while walking in the **entrance procession** and in the recessional, while the **Gospel** is **proclaimed**, and during **solemn blessings**. He may also hold it while giving the **homily** and at other times determined by the **rubrics** or by custom.

Paten   The name for the plate which holds the Eucharistic **bread** during **Mass**. Although the term is associated with a small, disk-like plate sized to hold only one large **host** for the **priest**, it can also be applied to a larger plate containing a sufficient amount of bread for the communion of the entire **assembly**. It is preferable to use only one large plate as a **sign** of the unity of the assembly and the offering of one **sacrifice**. A large paten would still be distinguished from a **ciborium**, however, in that a paten more resembles a plate, dish, or tray, whereas a ciborium resembles a cup or a bowl.

Paul VI, Pope (1897–1978)   Born Giovanni Battista Montini and elected pope in 1963. He continued the Second Vatican Council convened by **Pope John XXIII**, and promulgated its documents. He also approved and promulgated all the liturgical **rites** revised at the mandate of the Council. He was beatified in 2014.

Pectoral Cross   A **cross** worn by **bishops** in the **Roman Rite**. It is suspended from a chain worn around the neck and rests on the chest (in **Latin**, *pectus*). Some Russian **priests** also wear a pectoral cross, and many Eastern bishops wear a pectoral **icon** rather than a cross. At **Mass**, the pectoral cross is usually worn under the **chasuble**, although some bishops wear it outside the chasuble.

Penance   (1) The **sacrament** by which the baptized, through the mercy of God, receive pardon for their sins and reconciliation with the **Church** (see *Catechism of the Catholic Church*, 1422). This sacrament is most commonly **celebrated** by the private confession of sin and expression of sorrow by a **penitent** to a **confessor**, who then offers **absolution**. It is also commonly called **confession** or the Sacrament of **Reconciliation**.

(2) An act of **satisfaction**, or atonement, imposed on a penitent by the confessor as part of the Sacrament of Penance. See **Act of Penance**.

Penitent   A person who, in sorrow for his or her sins, participates in the **Sacrament** of **Penance** to receive sacramental **absolution**. The term can also be applied in general to anyone who is doing **penance**.

Penitential Act   The short **ritual** expression of sinfulness that normally takes place as part of the **Introductory Rites** of the **Mass**. The **rite** has three options: the first is a **confession**, usually called the **Confiteor**, recited by the **priest** and the **assembly** together; the second option consists of two **psalm** verses said by the priest with **responses** by the assembly; and the third option incorporates the **Kyrie** into spoken or sung **invocations** to **Christ**. It is omitted whenever the rite of **blessing** and sprinkling **water** takes place, when another liturgical action is joined to the beginning of Mass (such as the reception of **children** for **Baptism**), and on **Ash Wednesday**.

Penitential Rite (Scrutiny)   (1) The second step in the Christian initiation of unbaptized **children** who have reached **catechetical age**, found in the *Rite of Christian Initiation of Adults*. One or more penitential rites, which are similar to the scrutinies but simplified for children, may be **celebrated** during the period of final preparation for the celebration of the **sacraments of initiation**. These **rites** are celebrated within a **Liturgy of the Word** and may include an **anointing** with the **oil of catechumens**. **Penance** may be celebrated at the same liturgy with baptized children who are receiving the sacrament for the first time.

(2) An optional **rite** that may be celebrated with baptized but previously uncatechized **adults** who are in the final stages of preparing to receive the **sacraments** of **Confirmation** and **Eucharist**, or who are preparing to be received into the full communion of the Catholic **Church**. It is adapted from the rites of **scrutiny** for the **elect** and is similar in format, although the penitential rite does not include a prayer of **exorcism** because of the **candidates'** status as baptized. It is one of the rites adapted for use in the United States with uncatechized, baptized adults; it appears only in the US edition of the *Rite of Christian Initiation of Adults.*

Penitential Services Gatherings of the faithful centered on God's Word that inspires in them conversion and renewal of life. The structure of the **liturgy** follows that of the celebration of the **Word of God** as given in the **Rite** for **Reconciliation** of Several **Penitents** but without sacramental **absolution**.

Pentecost The fiftieth and final day of **Easter Time**; the eighth **Sunday** of Easter Time. Pentecost commemorates the descent of the Holy Spirit on the disciples as narrated in Acts 2:1–12. The celebration of Easter concludes with **Evening Prayer** on Pentecost and **Ordinary Time** resumes the next day.

Pentecost Vigil The celebration of **Mass** in the form of a prolonged **vigil** on the Saturday evening before **Pentecost Sunday**. The character of the Pentecost Vigil is one of urgent prayer, following the example of the **Apostles** and disciples, who persevered together with Mary, the Mother of Jesus, in awaiting the Holy Spirit. At such a vigil, after a prayer that concludes the **Introductory Rites**, the **priest** gives a brief exhortation introducing the **Liturgy of the Word**. Four Old Testament readings are then **proclaimed**, each followed by a **responsorial psalm** and a prayer, after which the **Glory to God in the Highest** is sung and the **collect** is prayed. The New Testament reading is then proclaimed, and Mass continues as usual.

People of God All those who belong to the **Church** through faith in **Christ** and **Baptism** (*Catechism of the Catholic Church*, 782). The liturgical **assembly** is described as "the People of God arrayed hierarchically" in the *General Instruction of the Roman Missal*, 16.

Perpetual Eucharistic Adoration Adoration of the **Blessed Sacrament**, either in the **tabernacle** or, more usually, exposed in a **monstrance**, that takes place essentially continuously. The setting for this devotion is a small **chapel**, not the main **altar** of a parish **church**. At least one person should be prayerfully present at all times so that the exposed Blessed Sacrament is never unattended. If **Mass** is to be **celebrated** where **exposition** takes place, the Blessed Sacrament is reposed during the celebration.

Petition (1) To request a particular outcome or favor from God in prayer.

(2) A statement or prayer within a **liturgy** that requests a particular outcome or favor from God. It can especially refer to the specific intentions or **intercessions** that are announced in the **Universal Prayer** at **Mass**, or as part of the intercessions in the **Liturgy of the Hours**.

Pew One of the long benches in **churches** that provide seating for the **assembly**.

Phos Hilaron The major song of praise sung during **Evening Prayer** in the **Byzantine Rite**. It is a praise of God as the light of the world, and usually is sung immediately after the Entrance of **Vespers**. It is usually translated as "O Gladsome Light."

Polyphony Term that refers to two or more singers (or groups of singers) singing individual parts at the same time.

Pontifical (1) In the singular, it is a common reference to the *Roman Pontifical*.

(2) In the plural, *pontificals* refers to the distinctive accessories normally worn or used by a **bishop,** such as the **pectoral cross,** the ring, the **miter,** and the **crosier.**

Pontifical Mass   A solemn **Mass celebrated** by a **bishop** according to the norms described in the *Ceremonial of Bishops*.

Postbaptismal Catechesis   **Mystagogical catechesis,** instruction given to the newly baptized, or **neophytes,** to help them deepen their understanding of the faith primarily through reflection on the **sacraments** they **celebrated** at **Easter.** It is also another name for the period of **mystagogy,** the final stage or period in the process of the *Rite of Christian Initiation of Adults*.

Praenotanda   The introductory texts in a **ritual** book, such as the *General Instruction of the Roman Missal*. Such texts usually have the title "Introduction" or "General Introduction" and provide important theological foundations and explanations for the ritual, along with norms, **rubrics,** and other instructions.

Prayer after Communion   One of the **presidential prayers** in the **Mass.** It is said after the distribution of **Holy Communion** and the period of **silence** or **hymn** of praise that follows, concluding the **Liturgy of the Eucharist.** The announcements and other elements of the **Concluding Rites** follow the prayer after communion.

Prayer of the Faithful   Another name for the **Universal Prayer** or **Bidding Prayers** during the celebration of the **Eucharist.**

Prayer of the Penitent   Prayer said by the **penitent** as part of the celebration of the **Sacrament** of **Penance.** The prayer expresses the penitent's sorrow and intention to avoid sin in the future. The prayer may take any one of several forms of varying length suggested by the **rite.**

Prayer over the Offerings One of the **presidential prayers** in the **Mass**. It is said at the conclusion of the **preparation of the gifts** and immediately precedes the **Eucharistic Prayer**.

Prayer over the People A prayer of **blessing** addressed to God that may immediately precede an expanded formula of blessing at the end of **Mass**. *The Roman Missal* contains prayers over the people for **Ash Wednesday** and the Sundays of **Lent**, optional texts for other weekdays of Lent, and forms for general use throughout the **liturgical year** and on the feasts of **saints**, which may be used at the discretion of the **presider**.

Prayers after Death A section of prayers and selections from Scripture found in the **ritual** books *Pastoral Care of the Sick: Rites of Anointing and Viaticum* and the *Order of Christian Funerals*. The texts may be used by a **priest**, **deacon**, or **lay minister** immediately following the death of a person or when the minister first meets with a family shortly after the death of a loved one. A priest is not to administer the **Sacrament** of the **Anointing of the Sick** to one who is already dead, but instead should use these prayers.

Prayers at the Foot of the Altar The **Introductory Rites** of the Roman **Mass** in the **Order** of Mass as **celebrated** according to the Missals published immediately after the **Council of Trent** and prior to the Missal resulting from the Second Vatican Council. They consist of an alternating recitation of part of **Psalm** 43 and a double recitation of the **Confiteor** said while standing at the foot of the **altar** steps; the prayers were recited inaudibly and were never considered a public part of the **liturgy**. These prayers were transformed into the public **Penitential Act** in the **Order** of Mass in the postconciliar *Roman Missal*.

Preaching   The act of giving a formal religious speech. There are different kinds of preaching. A **homily** refers to preaching done during a liturgical **service** by ordained **ministers** that is integrally connected to the liturgical action; it is based on the Scripture readings, the texts of the **liturgy**, or the particular celebration. A **sermon** is a religious exhortation or instruction that is thematic and not related to the readings or liturgy of the day.

Precatechumenate   A period of indeterminate length that precedes acceptance into the **order of catechumens**. In the *Rite of Christian Initiation of Adults* this time is called the period of **evangelization and precatechumenate**; it is also sometimes referred to as **inquiry**.

Preces   Intercessory prayers, often in the form of a **litany**. In the **Liturgy of the Hours**, the **intercessions** ending **Morning Prayer** and **Evening Prayer** are sometimes called *preces*.

Precious Blood   The **wine** that has been **consecrated** and has become the Blood of **Christ**.

Preconium (or Paschal Preconium or Praeconium)
An alternative name for the **Exsultet**.

Predella   The platform or step on which an **altar** is set in many churches.

Preface   The first section of the **Eucharistic Prayer**, starting with the **Introductory Dialogue** and ending with the **Sanctus (Holy, Holy, Holy)**. It **proclaims** the motives for giving thanks to God in this particular celebration, and therefore it is often **proper** to a particular liturgical **season** or day. The name is derived from a **Latin** word for "proclamation." It is part of the Eucharistic Prayer, not an introduction to it, as its name in English might suggest.

Preparation of the Gifts   The first section of the **Liturgy of the Eucharist**, during which the **altar** is prepared with the items that will be needed for that part of the **Mass**; sometimes referred to as the **offertory**, from its name in the Tridentine Missal. It begins with the **bread** and **wine** being brought in **procession** to the altar. The **priest** prepares the **gifts** with the prescribed prayers, washes his hands, and prays the **prayer over the offerings**, which concludes the **rite**. This section ritualizes the *taking* action of the **fourfold Eucharistic actions** of taking, **blessing**, breaking, and giving.

Preparation Rites   Various **rites** that can be **celebrated** with the **elect** on **Holy Saturday** in proximate preparation for the celebration of the **sacraments of initiation** at the **Easter Vigil** that evening. Some or all of the preparation rites given in the *Rite of Christian Initiation of Adults* may be celebrated: the presentation of the **Lord's Prayer**, if it has not already taken place; the "return" or recitation of the **Creed**; the **ephphetha** rite; and the choosing of a baptismal name.

Presbyter   A term derived from the Greek word for "elder." It describes the second **order** in the **Sacrament** of **Holy Orders**, more commonly referred to as *priest*.

Presbyterate   A term used for the **order** of priesthood, stemming from the term *presbyter*.

Presbyterium   The area where **priests** normally exercise their ministry in a **church** building. It includes the area around the **altar** and the area where the **presidential chair** and seats for **concelebrants** are located. In common use, *presbyterium* and *sanctuary* are interchangeable, although technically the sanctuary includes the **presbyterium**, the **ambo**, and in some churches, a **lectern** for the **cantor**.

Presence of Christ   As stated in the *Constitution on the Sacred Liturgy* and in subsequent documents on the **liturgy**, **Christ** is present in a variety of modes when the **Church** gathers for **worship**. Christ is present in the **assembly** gathered; in the person of the **priest** presiding; in the Word that is **proclaimed**; and in the **sacraments** that are **celebrated**, most especially in the **Eucharist**. These presences of Christ do not compete with each other but are different modes or actualizations of his one continuous presence. The Eucharistic presence is spoken of as **Real Presence** not because the other modes are not real, but because there is a unique, substantial presence par excellence in the **Blessed Sacrament**.

Presentations   **Rites** whereby the **Church** entrusts the **Creed** and the **Lord's Prayer**, the ancient texts that express the heart of the Church's faith, to the **elect**. The Creed is presented during the week following the first **scrutiny**; the actual presentation occurs when the **celebrant** and the **assembly** recite the Creed as the elect stand before them and listen. During the **Preparation Rites** on **Holy Saturday**, the elect will return, or recite, the Creed. The Lord's Prayer is presented during the week following the third scrutiny; the actual presentation occurs in the proclamation of the Matthew 6:9–13, in which our Lord teaches his followers how to pray. The presentations preferably take place during **Mass**. For pastoral reasons, they may be **celebrated** during the period of the **catechumenate**; the presentation of the **Lord's Prayer** may also take place during the **Preparation Rites** on Holy Saturday.

Presidential Prayers   The prayers that the **priest celebrant** prays audibly in the name of the entire **assembly**: the **Eucharistic Prayer**, the **collect**, the **prayer over the offerings**, and the **prayer after communion**. The last three are collectively called the **orations**. In his role as celebrant, the **priest** audibly prays the prayer that concludes the **Universal Prayer**, so this also may be considered one of the presidential prayers.

Presider   The title frequently given to the **priest celebrant** at a celebration of the **Eucharist** or other **liturgy**. Its first use seems to be by **Justin Martyr,** and it emphasizes his unique role in the liturgical **assembly** within the celebration of the Eucharist. It differs from the term **celebrant** in that, while, in a broad sense, everyone in the assembly **celebrates** the liturgy and the **concelebrating** priests also celebrate the **Mass,** only one person in the assembly can preside. Hence, *main celebrant* and *principal celebrant* are used synonymously with the term *presider.* Additionally, when a **bishop** is present at Mass but a priest is celebrating the Mass, the bishop is said to preside over the celebration.

Presidential Chair   The chair reserved for use by the presiding **priest** at a **liturgy**. It signifies "his function of presiding over the gathering and of directing the prayer" (GIRM, 31). The presidential chair is one of three focal points in the **sanctuary,** along with the **altar** and the **ambo.** During **Mass,** the presiding priest should be at the chair during the **Introductory Rites,** the **Liturgy of the Word,** and the **Concluding Rites.** He may also give the **homily** standing at the presidential chair.

Prie-Dieu   See kneeler.

Priest   The second **order** of **ministry** in the **Sacrament of Holy Orders,** also called a *presbyter. Priest* is a translation of the **Latin** *sacerdos* and the Greek *hiereus*; *presbyter* is a Latin word, a close transliteration of the Greek *presbuteros,* meaning "elder." Through **ordination,** the priest is authorized to **preside** at **Mass** and exercise his proper role in the celebration of all the **sacraments.** Technically, there is only one priest, Jesus **Christ** (Hebrews 2:18, 4:14), and both presbyters and **bishops** share in Christ's priesthood when they preside at the **altar.** Thus, when the official liturgical texts speak about priests, they frequently mean both presbyters and bishops. In addition, all Christians participate in the priesthood of Christ by their **Baptism,** forming a "royal priesthood" (1 Peter 2:9).

Priesthood of the Faithful   The share in the priesthood of **Christ** that all Christians receive as a result of their **Baptism**, also called the **Baptismal Priesthood**. Because of their Baptism, the faithful truly offer **sacrifice** to God through their lives and their prayers (cf. 1 Peter 2:5, 9). This is distinguished from the **ministerial priesthood** conferred through the **Sacrament** of **Holy Orders**.

Procession   Any formal movement of one or more persons from one place to another during the **Mass** and other liturgies. The most solemn processions are led by a **thurifer**, who is immediately followed by a **cross bearer** between two **ministers** with **candles**. A typical Mass may include several processions: at the **Entrance**, at the **Gospel**, at the **preparation of the gifts**, at **communion**, and following the **dismissal**.

Procession with the Gifts   The bringing forward of the **bread** and **wine** by members of the **assembly** at the beginning of the **Liturgy of the Eucharist**. Monetary **offerings** for the **Church** and for the poor often are brought forward at this time as well. Through this rite the people symbolically present themselves along with the **gifts** of bread and wine that will be transformed and then received back as the Body and Blood of Christ.

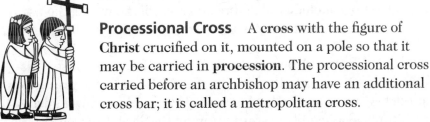

Processional Cross   A **cross** with the figure of **Christ** crucified on it, mounted on a pole so that it may be carried in **procession**. The processional cross carried before an archbishop may have an additional cross bar; it is called a metropolitan cross.

Proclaim   To read the Scripture readings out loud during a **liturgy** in a manner that is reverent, appropriate to a public forum, assured, and intelligible. A liturgical proclamation of Scripture conveys the meaning of the passage, professes that what is being read is true, and invites the hearers to respond in faith.

Profession of Faith   The formula that expresses what the **Church** believes about God. It is also referred to as the **Symbol** or the **Creed**. At **Mass**, if required, the Profession of Faith occurs after the **homily**, and it usually takes the form of the **Niceno-Constantinopolitan Creed**, though the **Apostles' Creed** may also be used, especially during **Lent** and **Easter Time**. On some occasions, such as the celebration of **Baptism** and **Confirmation**, the Profession of Faith is in a question-and-answer form.

Profession (Religious Profession)   The **rite** of taking vows by members of religious institutes. The rite is found in the *Roman Ritual* or in the special ritual books of the various religious institutes; *The Roman Missal* provides **Mass** formularies for these occasions.

Progressive Solemnity   The principle that guides the choices concerning what should be sung in a **liturgy**. The fullest, most solemn form, everything that demands singing would be sung; the simplest form would involve no singing at all. In between are various degrees of how much will be sung, stemming from the nature of the celebration. Considerations regarding the degree of solemnity include the **time** of the **liturgical year,** the day of the week, and the rank of the day on which the celebration takes place. Other considerations include the nature and style of the music, the use of various instruments, and which parts of the **rite** will be sung.

Profound Bow   A **bow** of the body; a bow from the waist. This type of bow is made to the **altar** by the **ministers** in the **procession** at the beginning and end of **Mass** and in general whenever anyone in the liturgical **assembly** passes in front of the altar. Everyone in the liturgical assembly makes a profound bow during the **Creed**, in recognition of the Incarnation. There are also prescribed times in the **liturgy** when the **priest** and the **deacon** make profound bows.

Proper   Those texts in the **Mass** and in the **Liturgy of the Hours** that are particular to a given day. The complete proper for Mass includes the **entrance antiphon**, **communion antiphon**, readings, **orations**, and **preface**. The proper is distinguished from the **ordinary** and the **common**.

Psalm   A text from the Old Testament Book of Psalms, which is a collection of songs, most of which were composed for **worship**. Psalms are frequently sung in the **liturgy** while **processions** take place. A **responsorial psalm** is sung after the **first reading** during the **Liturgy of the Word**, and psalms make up a major portion of the **Liturgy of the Hours**.

Psalmist   The liturgical **minister** who leads the singing of the **responsorial psalm** at **Mass**. Sometimes this role is combined with that of the **cantor**.

Psalmody   The section within each of the hours in the **Liturgy of the Hours** where the **psalms** are sung or recited. For some of the hours, the psalmody comprises only psalms; for others, the psalmody is composed of psalms and a **canticle**.

Psalter   (1) The Book of **Psalms** itself.
   (2) The body of psalms that are used in the **Liturgy of the Hours**, and a book that contains all these psalms.

Pulpit   An alternative name for an **ambo** or **lectern**.

Purification (Purify)   The cleansing of liturgical vessels to remove any trace of the **consecrated** Eucharistic **elements**; formerly called the **ablutions**. This cleansing may be performed by a **priest**, **deacon**, or **instituted acolyte** after communion or after **Mass**. This cleansing is different from the ordinary washing of vessels for cleanliness, which takes place after Mass, after the purification is completed.

Purification and Enlightenment   The final prebaptismal period of the catechumenal process for **adults** preparing for initiation in the Catholic **Church**. It is a time of intense spiritual preparation marked by the celebration of the **scrutinies** and the **presentations**. It usually coincides with **Lent**. It begins with the **Rite of Election** and ends with the celebration of the **sacraments of initiation**, usually at the **Easter Vigil**. Those who are in this stage are called the *elect*, also *competentes* or *illuminandi*.

Purificator   The cloth used to wipe the rim of the **chalice** containing the Blood of **Christ** after someone drinks from it during the celebration of the **Eucharist**. The purificator is usually rectangular in shape, folded lengthwise in thirds and then in half, and embroidered with a small red **cross**.

Pyx   A vessel used to carry **consecrated bread** for **Holy Communion** to the sick.

Quinceañera   A celebration observed around the time of a girl's fifteenth birthday in many Latin American countries and many Latin American communities in the United States. The celebration marks the passage from childhood to young womanhood; it usually includes a **Mass** or **Liturgy of the Word**. The **United States Conference of Catholic Bishops** publishes an *Order for the Blessing on the Fifteenth Birthday* and *Fifteen Questions on the Quinceañera*.

R

RCIA   Abbreviation for the *Rite of Christian Initiation of Adults*.

Reader   The liturgical **minister** who **proclaims** the readings before the **Gospel** during the **Liturgy of the Word**; often referred to as a **lector**, although *lector* is more correctly used if the person has been formally instituted in that ministry. The reader proclaims the appointed Scripture passage at the **ambo**. Ideally there is a different reader for each reading, to highlight the uniqueness and importance of each reading and to lend greater dignity to the proclamation of the **Word of God**. In the absence of a **deacon**, the reader may also announce the **petitions** in the **Universal Prayer**. Readers should be commissioned using the Order for the **Blessing** of Readers in the *Book of Blessings*.

Real Presence   Theological term referring to the **mystery** that the **Lord** Jesus **Christ** is truly present in the **Eucharist** under the appearances of **bread** and **wine**. It is the whole Christ who is present, Body and Blood, soul and divinity. Once the bread and wine have been **consecrated**, the Real Presence endures permanently as long as the **species** of bread and wine remain.

Reception of Baptized Christians into the Full Communion of the Catholic Church
The liturgical **rite** used to receive into the full communion of the Catholic **Church** an **adult** who was validly baptized in a non-Catholic Christian Church. The rite usually takes place during **Mass**, after the **homily**. The rite consists of an invitation, a **profession of faith** made by the **candidate**, the act of reception by the **priest celebrant**, the celebration of **Confirmation**, a **sign** of welcome, **intercessions**, and a **sign of peace**; the newly received Catholic partakes in the **Eucharist** at the same Mass.

Priests who receive a baptized non-Catholic into the full communion of the Catholic **Church** automatically have the **faculty** to confirm that person. In the case of Eastern Christians who enter the Catholic Church, no liturgical rite is required, only a simple profession of Catholic faith.

Recognitio   The statement of approval or acceptance given by the **Apostolic See** that authorizes certain documents adopted by an **ecclesial** body, such as a conference of **bishops**. Translations of liturgical texts must receive the *recognitio* before they are implemented.

Reconciliation   An action of healing relationships wounded in some way; used in a liturgical sense to refer to the reestablishment of a right relationship between God and the human race through the life, Death, and Resurrection of Jesus **Christ**. The term is commonly used as a title for the **Sacrament** of **Penance**, or **confession**.

Reconciliation Room (Chapel)   The place where the **Sacrament** of **Penance** is **celebrated** according to the reformed **rite** of the Second Vatican Council. A **reconciliation** room affords the **penitent** the opportunity to **celebrate** the sacrament either face-to-face with the **priest** or behind a screen or curtain, which distinguishes it from a **confessional**.

Red   The **liturgical color** used on **Palm Sunday of the Lord's Passion**, on **Good Friday**, on **Pentecost** Sunday, on celebrations of the Lord's **Passion**, on the **feast** days of **Apostles** and Evangelists, in **Votive Masses** of the Most **Precious Blood** of our Lord Jesus **Christ** and of the Holy Spirit, and on celebrations of **martyrs**.

Redemptionis Sacramentum   Instruction on the **Eucharist**, *On Certain Matters to Be Observed or to Be Avoided Regarding the Most Holy Eucharist*, issued in 2004 by the **Congregation for Divine Worship and the Discipline of the Sacraments**. The document, which includes prescriptions of a juridical nature, addresses issues pertaining to the correct celebration of the Eucharist, noting some particular abuses and clarifying other **proper** procedures to be followed.

Reformation   The period of historical events in the sixteenth century that led to divisions in Western Christianity and the establishment of independent Protestant **churches**. One of the major leaders of the Reformation was **Martin Luther** in Germany.

Regina Caeli   An **antiphon** in honor of the Blessed Virgin Mary, used during **Easter Time** at the end of **Night Prayer** and during the day in place of the Angelus.

Register of Catechumens   The book in which the names of those unbaptized **adults** who have been a accepted as **catechumens** is recorded. The names of the **sponsors** and the **minister** and the date and place of the celebration of the **Rite** of Acceptance into the **order of catechumens** should also be recorded. Each parish should have a register of catechumens.

Relic   Pieces of bone or other part of the body of a **saint**. This type of relic, a first-class relic, is the only type that may be placed in an **altar**. The presence of relics within an altar or altar stone is optional. These relics should preferably be recognizable as parts of human bodies; they are to be placed under the altar, rather than in a niche carved into the altar top. Second-class relics (something owned or used by the saint) and third-class relics (something touched to a first-class relic) may be used to venerate the **saints**.

Reliquary   A container for **relics**.

Renunciation of Sin   The **ritual** questioning that precedes the **Profession of Faith** made at **Baptism** or in the renewal of Baptism. There are two forms of the formula for the renunciation of sin, each of which consists of three questions that center on the rejection of Satan and his works.

Reposition   The liturgical action of returning the exposed **Blessed Sacrament** to the **tabernacle** after a period of **adoration** and, often, **Benediction**.

Reredos   The altarpiece or screen behind the **altar**, especially if the altar is attached to a wall, as was customary until 1964. The reredos is frequently decorated with paintings, **statues**, or other artistic elements.

Reservation Chapel   A separate **chapel** integrated with, but distinct from, the main body of the **church** in which is housed the **tabernacle** containing the reserved **Blessed Sacrament**.

Responses   The answers made by the **assembly** to the various prayers, **greetings**, and proclamations of Scripture during the celebration of any **liturgy**.

Responsorial   The type of **chanting**, usually of a **psalm**, in which a soloist sings the verses while the **choir** or **assembly** sings a response, usually after each verse.

Responsorial Psalm   The **psalm** that is sung or recited after the **first reading** in a **liturgy**; also called the **Gradual**. It is normally **proclaimed** responsorially, with a **psalmist** singing the text of the psalm and the **assembly** responding with a response usually taken from a verse of the same psalm.

Responsory   The verses, usually taken from the **psalms**, used as a response to the Scripture reading during the celebration of one of the hours of the **Liturgy of the Hours**.

Ring   (1) A ring, frequently with a jewel, is worn by a **Roman Rite bishop** on the ring finger of his right hand. It is given to the bishop at his episcopal **ordination**, and it symbolizes his **marriage** to the diocese.

(2) Rings are blessed and given at the celebration of **matrimony**. The **rite** presupposes that rings will be worn by both the husband and the wife.

Rite (1) The title of any official liturgical ceremony, such as the *Rite of Christian Initiation of Adults*. The term is sometimes interchangeable with the words *order* or *ordo*, as in the *Order of Mass* or *Order of Christian Funerals*.

(2) A section of a larger ceremony, such as the **Introductory Rites** or the **Concluding Rites** of the **Mass**.

(3) A **ritual** family usually associated with a particular territory, which includes the individual traditions, feasts, **canon** law, ways of celebrating the sacraments, and approaches to theology. The two major rites in the Catholic **Church** are the **Roman Rite** and the **Byzantine Rite** (also used by Orthodox Christians).

Rite of Baptism for Children

The **ritual** book, part of the *Roman Ritual*, that gives the **rites** for the **Baptism** of **children** who have not yet attained the age of discretion (the age of reason), presumed to be about age seven. It includes ritual for bringing a child who is already baptized, usually in an emergency situation, to the church, often referred to as "supplying the ceremonies."

Rite of Christian Initiation of Adults (RCIA)

The **ritual** book, part of the *Roman Ritual*, that gives the norms, directives, and ritual celebrations for initiating unbaptized **adults** and **children** who have reached **catechetical age** into **Christ** and incorporating them into the **Church**. The RCIA prescribes a sequence of periods, or stages (**Evangelization and Precatechumenate, Catechumenate, Purification and Enlightenment,** and **Postbaptismal Catechesis**), and rites by which **candidates** transition from one stage to another (Acceptance into the **Order of Catechumens; Rite of Election**), which culminate in the celebration of the **sacraments of initiation,** usually at the **Easter Vigil**. The RCIA also includes an adapted process for completing the Christian initiation of baptized but uncatechized Catholics and for bringing baptized but uncatechized non-Catholics into the full communion of the Catholic Church.

Rite of Committal   The last liturgical act in the funeral rites, found in the *Order of Christian Funerals*. It is an expression of hope that the deceased will share in the glory of the resurrection and is the final leave-taking by the mourners. The **rite** may take place at the grave, at the crematorium, or in a cemetery **chapel**; it may also be used for burial at sea. The rite includes a short Scripture verse, a prayer over the place of committal, the committal itself, **intercessions**, the **Lord's Prayer**, a concluding prayer, and a **prayer over the people**. It may be **celebrated** by a **priest**, **deacon**, or **lay minister**.

Rite of Confirmation   The **ritual** book, part of the *Roman Pontifical* that contains the **rites** for the celebration of the **Sacrament** of **Confirmation** when it is conferred apart from **Baptism**.

Rite of Election   The second step for unbaptized **adults** preparing for the **sacraments of initiation**, also called the **Enrollment of Names**. The **rite** closes the period of the **catechumenate** and marks the beginning of the period of **Purification and Enlightenment**, which usually corresponds to **Lent**. With this rite the **Church** makes its election of the **catechumens** to receive the sacraments. The **bishop** is the usual **celebrant** at the Rite of Election; he asks the **godparents**, and possibly the whole community, to give testimony to the readiness of the catechumens. He invites the catechumens to enroll their names in the **Book of the Elect** and declare them to be members of the elect. The Rite of Election normally takes place on or near the First **Sunday** of Lent.

Rite of Peace   The section of the **Mass** that immediately follows the **doxology** after the **Lord's Prayer**. It consists of a prayer said audibly by the presiding **priest** ("Lord Jesus **Christ**, who said to your Apostles . . . ") with the people's **response**, followed by a **greeting** with its response, and the invitation to exchange the **sign of peace**.

Rite of Penance   The **ritual** book, part of the *Roman Ritual*, that provides the **rites** for the celebration of the **Sacrament** of **Penance**. Included are the Rite of **Reconciliation** of Individual **Penitents**, the Rite of Reconciliation of Several Penitents with Individual **Confession** and Absolution, the Rite for Reconciliation of Several Penitents with General Confession and Absolution, and sample **penitential services**.

Rites of Ordination of a Bishop, of Priests, and of Deacons
The **ritual** book, part of the *Roman Pontifical*, used for the **ordination** of **bishops**, **priests**, and **deacons**. The first edition of these **rites** following the Second Vatican Council was issued in 1968, with a revision in 1989. The current English translation was introduced in 2003. The book also includes the Rite of Admission to Candidacy for **Holy Orders**.

Ritual   (1) A formalized action. In general, *ritual* can refer to any human activity that marks a significant moments through expected and repeated patterns of behavior. Secular rituals include folk dancing, sports customs (shaking hands with or bowing to an opponent, for example), and birthday traditions. Both secular and religious rituals include rules, repeated behavior by key figures, and expectations by the participants.

   (2) In a religious context, *ritual* refers to special activities of an established group with a common belief system. These activities have a set structure and employ **symbols** and words that express the beliefs of the group.

   (3) In a Catholic context, when referencing a specific book, *ritual* usually indicates a section of the *Roman Ritual* containing rites for the celebration of a **sacrament** or other liturgical **rite**.

Ritual Masses   A category of **Mass** formularies found in *The Roman Missal* to be used when **sacraments** and other **rituals** are celebrated within Mass. Examples include Masses for the Conferral of the **sacraments of initiation**, for the Conferral of the **Anointing of the Sick**, and for **Religious Profession**.

Rochet   A white linen **vestment**, similar to a **surplice**, worn by **bishops** and other prelates.

Rogation Days   Before the liturgical reforms of the Second Vatican Council, Rogation Days were three days of special prayer and **intercession** in the calendar of the Tridentine Missal that came before **Ascension** Thursday. Currently, they are spoken of together with **Ember Days** as special liturgical days where the **Church** asks the **Lord** for particular needs and gives thanks to God publicly. **Conferences of bishops** are to arrange the time and manner of celebrating Ember and Rogation Days.

Roman Canon   The name given to **Eucharistic Prayer** I in *The Roman Missal*. It was the only Eucharistic Prayer (with minor changes) used in the Roman **Church** before the Second Vatican Council since at least around the time of Pope **Gregory the Great** (590–604).

Roman Missal   The book or books containing the prayers, **hymns**, and Scripture readings prescribed for the celebration of **Mass**. Before the revision of the Missal in 1570, after the **Council of Trent**, the various texts were found in different books, but these were combined into one volume after the Council. The one volume Missal was commonplace until the Second Vatican Council. The present-day Missal, published in 1970 and currently in its third edition, is subdivided into several books: a book of prayers used by the **priest**, which is still called the "Missal" even though technically the book contains only part of the Missal; the **Lectionary**, which contains the Scripture readings; and the book of **hymns** and **antiphons** called the **Gradual**.

Roman Pontifical   The book that contains **rites** normally celebrated by a **bishop** in the **Roman Rite**, such as **Confirmation**, ordinations, and the **Dedication of a Church** and an Altar.

Roman Rite   The **ritual** system used by the **Bishop** of Rome, the pope, and those associated with that tradition. It is noted for its starkness, simplicity, practicality, sobriety, and dignity. It is in marked contrast with other **rites** in the Catholic **Church**, such as the **Byzantine Rite**, whose ceremonies are marked by the use of much symbolism and repetition.

Roman Ritual   The title encompassing all the individual **ritual** books that contain the prayers and **rites** for the celebrations of the **sacraments**, other liturgies, and **blessings**. In general, the *Roman Ritual* contains all the rites except **Mass**, which is found in *The Roman Missal*; the **Liturgy of the Hours**, also called the **Divine Office**; and those used primarily by a **bishop**, which are found in the *Roman Pontifical*. Prior to the revision of the **rites** after the Second Vatican Council, the entire *Roman Ritual* was contained in one book.

Rood Screen   A screen or wall that separated the **choir** section of a **church** from the **nave** in some medieval-style churches. Doorways corresponding to the aisles in the church allowed the passage between the choir and the nave. Frequently the screen was surmounted by a **cross** (rood) over the center passageway.

Rosary   A devotion consisting of prescribed sets of prayers said in a repeated pattern while meditating on events in the lives of **Christ** and his mother. These events, referred to as mysteries, are arranged in four sets of five: Joyful (related to the Incarnation and the childhood of Christ); Luminous (related to Christ's active ministry); Sorrowful (related to Christ's Passion); and Glorious (related to Christ's Resurrection and Mary's sharing in Christ's risen life). The prayers are usually counted by means of a set of prayer beads, also called a rosary. A rosary usually consists of a circle of 54 beads to which is attached a strand with five beads and a **crucifix**. The 54 beads are arranged into five groups of ten, called decades, which are separated by a space and a larger bead. Each decade corresponds to one of the prescribed mysteries. While meditating on each of the mysteries, the **Hail Mary** is said ten times, using the ten beads to keep count. Each decade is preceded by the recitation of the **Lord's Prayer** and followed by the Glory Be. Pope John Paul II's encyclical

letter *Rosarium Virginis Mariae* (2002) gave new impetus to the **Rosary** and introduced the Luminous Mysteries.

Rose   The **liturgical color** that may be worn on the Third **Sunday** of **Advent** (**Gaudete Sunday**) and on the Fourth Sunday of **Lent** (**Laetare Sunday**).

Rubric   A direction or explanatory instruction printed between prayers or other spoken texts of a liturgical **rite**. The word *rubric* is derived from the **Latin** word for red because rubrics are normally printed in red in the liturgical books. Some rubrics are descriptive, and thus may be adapted in certain situations; and others are prescriptive, and thus must be carried out as written. Rubrics are meant to give structure and order to a **ritual**. The term is often used in the plural to speak of the norms or directives of a **liturgy** as a whole.

S

Sabbath The seventh day of the week, Saturday, observed by the Jewish people as a day of rest and prayer as commanded by God, commemorating the day on which God rested after creation (Exodus 20:8–11). For Christians, **Sunday**, the day on which **Christ** rose from the dead, is the day of **worship**. Although Sunday is sometimes referred to as the Sabbath day, this is inaccurate.

Sacrament In the most general definition, a visible **sign** of an invisible grace, as the *Catechism of the Council of Trent* says. Thus, the fundamental sacrament is **Christ**, the visible sign of God's presence on earth. Next is the **Church**, which, according to article 1 of *Lumen gentium*, is "a sacrament—a sign and instrument, that is, of communion with God."

    Most commonly, *sacrament* refers to seven specific **rituals**— **Baptism, Confirmation, Eucharist, Penance, Anointing of the Sick, Matrimony**, and **Holy Orders**—that are considered to have been instituted by Christ. Sacraments are frequently described by reference to a key material action or object (**matter**) that is joined to a specific liturgical text (**form**).

Sacrament of Reconciliation Another name for the **Sacrament** of **Penance**.

Sacramentals Sacred **signs**, including words, actions, and objects that signify spiritual effects achieved through the **intercession** of the Church. Unlike the **sacraments**, which have been instituted by **Christ**, sacramentals are instituted by the Church. Sacramentals include **blessings**, medals, **statues** and other sacred images, **palms, holy water**, and many devotions, including the **Rosary**. They prepare us to receive the fruit of the sacraments and **sanctify** different circumstances of life (see *Catechism of the Catholic Church*, 1677).

Sacramentary   A book containing prayers used by a **priest** or **bishop**, typically for the celebration of the **Mass**. Some ancient sacramentaries date to the sixth and seventh centuries (e.g., the Leonine, Gelasian, and Gregorian Sacramentaries) and contain prayers used at Mass and other **rites**. Around the thirteenth century, the prayers in sacramentaries were supplemented with **antiphons** usually sung by a **choir** and scriptural readings formerly found in lectionaries, to form a *Missale Plenum*, a full missal. Such a missal used at Rome was named ***The Roman Missal***. Between the late 1960s and the early 2000s, the book containing the prayers for the priest at Mass was, in some English-speaking countries, called the *Sacramentary*, because it did not contain any Scripture readings.

Sacraments of Initiation   The **Sacraments** of **Baptism**, **Confirmation**, and **Eucharist**. All three sacraments are necessary to be fully initiated into the **Church**. **Adults**, including **children** of **catechetical age**, receive all three sacraments in one **liturgy** when being initiated into the Church. Many Orthodox Christians and Eastern **Rite** Catholics administer all three sacraments together, even to infants, at the time of initiation.

Sacraments of Healing   The **Sacraments** of **Penance** and **Anointing of the Sick**, as described in the *Catechism of the Catholic Church*. Through the ministry of the Church, they continue the **Lord's** work of healing and salvation.

Sacraments of Vocation   The **Sacraments** of **Matrimony** and **Holy Orders**, also referred to in the *Catechism of the Catholic Church* as sacraments at the service of communion. These sacraments strengthen the recipients to live the mission conferred by their vocation and build up the **Church**.

Sacramentum Caritatis   The postsynodal apostolic exhortation on the **Eucharist** as the source and summit of the **Church's** life and mission issued by Pope Benedict XVI in 2007. The text discusses the relationship of the Eucharist to all the **sacraments**, the meaning of *ars celebrandi* (the art of celebration), the nature of participation at the celebration of the Eucharist, and connecting the Eucharist to the mission of living the Christian life.

Sacrarium   A special sink, usually with an attached cover, whose drain goes directly into the ground rather than into a sewer, found in the **sacristy** of a **church**. Its purpose is primarily the disposal of **water** used for cleansing the sacred vessels and other items that come in contact with the Eucharistic **elements**.

Sacrifice   A means by which human beings offer reverence to and establish communion with God. The English word is derived from the **Latin** *sacrificium*, itself derived from *sacer*, "set apart, holy," and *facere*, "to make." This term translates the Greek *thusia*, meaning "sacrifice" or "victim." In the Old Testament, sacrifice is frequently associated with the destruction of a victim, such as the burnt offering sacrifices of Cain and Abel, or the attempted sacrifice of Isaac by Abraham. However, in the **psalms**, praise and **thanksgiving** are considered to be sacrifices (Psalm 50:23, 116:17), and love and mercy, sacrifices of the heart, are considered more important than sacrifices and holocausts (Hosea 6:6). The **Mass** is a sacrifice in that it makes present the ultimate sacrifice of Jesus on the **Cross** (Hebrews 7:27, 9:12), but it is also a bloodless sacrifice of praise (Sirach 35:1–2) offered through the prayers, **hymns**, and lives of the **assembly**.

Sacristan   The liturgical **minister** who has the responsibility for preparing everything needed for liturgical celebrations. The duties of the sacristan include arranging everything needed before the **liturgy** begins, and cleaning up and putting things away after. Sometimes his or her duties include caring for the **sacristy**, **vestments**, vessels, and the good order of the **worship** space itself. The ministry of sacristan is included in the **Order** for the **Blessing** of **Altar Servers**, Sacristans, Musicians, and **Ushers** in the *Book of Blessings*.

Sacristy   The room in which **vestments** and liturgical items are stored and prepared for use before liturgies. It is also commonly used as a **vesting room**, although larger **churches** and **cathedrals** may have a separate vesting room, called the **secretarium**.

Sacrosanctum Concilium   The **Latin** title of the *Constitution on the Sacred Liturgy* of the Second Vatican Council. It was the first decree of the Council, promulgated on December 4, 1963. It allowed the celebration of liturgical **rites** in the **vernacular**, called for the full, conscious, and **active participation** of the **assembly**, and ordered the revision of all liturgical **rites**.

Saint   A person noted for holiness of life and heroic virtue. Technically, anyone who has entered into heaven is a saint, but only those recognized by the **Church** are honored in the **liturgy** and on the **liturgical calendar**. Before anyone can publicly be called a saint, there is a formal investigation into the person's background. When the cause of a particular person has been accepted in Rome, the person may be called Servant of God. When the formal process concludes, they are given the title Venerable. When miracles attributed to the **intercession** of the holy person are demonstrated, the Venerable becomes Blessed and, finally, Saint.

Salt   Salt may be used in **blessing holy water**. *The Roman Missal* includes as an option the blessing of salt, and the mixing of it with water that has also been blessed, as part of the blessing and sprinkling of holy **water** that may occur at the beginning of **Mass**.

Salve Regina   One of the **antiphons** in honor of the Blessed Virgin Mary that may be used at the end of **Night Prayer**. It is one of the oldest Marian antiphons in Western Christianity. The title comes from the first words of the prayer, "Hail, Holy Queen."

Sanctify   To make holy, or to **consecrate**.

Sanctoral Cycle   A term sometimes used to refer to the portions of the **liturgical calendar** pertaining to the **commemoration** of the **saints** or to celebrations of the **Lord** or of the Blessed Virgin Mary associated with specific dates (with the exceptions of Christmas and the Solemnity of Mary on January 1), such as the Transfiguration on

August 6. In contrast, the portion of the liturgical calendar pertaining to the liturgical **times** (**seasons**) is sometimes called the **temporal cycle**.

Sanctuary   The area of the **church** in which the **presidential chair**, **altar**, and **ambo** are located, and in which the primary **ministers** may also sit. Normally it is somewhat elevated, for the sake of visibility. It should be in some way distinct from the other areas of the church, yet at the same time integrally related to the entire space, to convey a sense of unity and wholeness. It is sometimes referred to as the **presbyterium** or **chancel**.

Sanctuary Lamp (or Light, or Candle)   The flame required to be kept burning near the **tabernacle** when the **Blessed Sacrament** is reserved, as a **sign** of honor for the **presence of Christ**. The lamp is to be either of oil or of wax.

Sanctus   The **Latin** name for the **acclamation** in the **Eucharistic Prayer** that begins, "Holy, Holy, Holy **Lord** God of hosts" ("Sanctus, Sanctus, Sanctus Dominus Deus Sabaoth"). It marks the end of the **preface** section of the Eucharistic Prayer.

Satisfaction   Atonement or making amends for a wrong or evil act one has done. In the **Sacrament** of **Penance**, this is accomplished by an **Act of Penance** as a **sign** of conversion and amendment of life, and as a way of rectifying the wrongdoing. The satisfaction should be seen as medicinal, to help the **penitent** be cured of the sickness of sin, and therefore, whenever possible, the remedy should correspond to the nature of the sin.

Schmemann, Alexander (1921–1983)   Orthodox liturgical theologian and author of numerous books. He attempted to synthesize the older style of **allegorical** reflection on the Byzantine liturgical **rites** with both a modern historical appreciation of the origin of these rites and contemporary theological reflection.

Schola Cantorum   Latin term (literally, "school of singers") sometimes used to refer to a **choir** that sings at a **liturgy**.

Scrutiny   A **rite** of self-searching and repentance intended to heal whatever is weak or sinful in the hearts of the **elect**, and to strengthen all that is good. Three scrutinies are normally **celebrated**—on the Third, Fourth, and Fifth **Sundays** of **Lent**—as the elect prepare for sacramental initiation at the **Easter Vigil**. The scrutinies are usually celebrated within Mass; they include **intercessions** for the elect, a prayer of **exorcism**, and the **laying on of hands**.

Seal of Confession   The inviolable obligation of the **priest** never to reveal anything of what he has heard from a **penitent** in the **Sacrament** of **Penance**.

Season (Liturgical)   See **time (liturgical)**.

Second Reading   On **Sundays** and certain major celebrations, a second reading is **proclaimed** after the **first reading** and the **responsorial psalm**. It is taken from one of the books of the New Testament other than the **Gospels**.

Secretarium   The **vesting room**, distinct from the **sacristy**, which is found in larger churches and **cathedrals**, from which the **entrance procession** begins.

Sedia Gestatoria   The portable papal throne on which the pope sat when he was carried in **procession** to the **altar** at major papal Masses. The *sedia* has not been used since Pope John Paul I in 1978.

Sending of the Catechumens for Election   An optional **rite** that may be **celebrated** before the **catechumens** take part in the **Rite of Election**. The rite, which usually takes place at **Mass**, expresses the parish community's approval and support of their election by the **bishop**. Depending on the practice of the diocese, the **Book of the Elect** may be signed by the catechumens at this **liturgy** and presented to the bishop at the Rite of Election.

Sequence   A poetic **hymn** sung before the **Gospel Acclamation** on certain days. Sequences are required on **Easter Sunday** and **Pentecost**; they are optional on the **Solemnity** of the Most Holy Body and Blood of the **Lord** and on the **Memorial** of Our Lady of Sorrows.

Seraphim   The highest **order** of **angels**, characterized by an intense love of the Holy Trinity.

Serapion   **Bishop** of Thmuis (Nile Delta) from around 339 until his death in about 362. A *Euchologion* (collection of prayers) is attributed to him, which contains many liturgical texts, including a developed **Eucharistic Prayer**. This seems to be the earliest evidence of the inclusion of the **Sanctus** in the Eucharistic Prayer.

Sermon   A religious or morally oriented speech, especially one not integrally connected with the liturgical action or occasion, that is, a talk given at the occasion of the **liturgy**, but not an essential part of it. The liturgical **preaching** done in the course of a liturgy is more correctly called a **homily**.

Serve   The term used to describe assistance given to the presiding **priest** at a **liturgy**. The **ministers** who assist the presiding priest in the **sanctuary** are frequently called **servers** and are said to "serve **Mass**." In the **Byzantine Rite**, the liturgical texts speak about a **priest** or **deacon** "serving the Divine Liturgy" rather than using the Western terminology of "celebrating."

Server   A common term for those who assist the presiding **priest** during the celebration of any **liturgy**, especially **Mass**. The official texts speak of "**acolytes**" and "**ministers**" in addition to "servers," but frequently the three terms are interchangeable in terms of actual duties one performs, although "acolyte" normally refers to someone instituted in the official ministry.

Service   A generic name for any public **worship**, more commonly used by non-Catholics. It is often used interchangeably with *liturgy*.

Sign   Anything that points to a meaning beyond itself. The meanings associated with signs are mainly literal or informative; they often take their meaning by common consent. For example, an octagon by convention and, eventually, adoption by law, has come to mean that one is required to stop, even though it has no inherent relationship to traffic or movement. Especially in liturgical use, *sign* is often distinguished from *symbol*. Symbols are understood to reveal deeper, even ultimate, meaning. Even so, the two terms are often used interchangeably.

Sign of Peace   The **ritual greeting** that takes place during the **Liturgy of the Eucharist**, before the **Fraction Rite**. The actual sign that is exchanged (for example, a handshake, a hug, a **bow**, a **kiss**) will vary greatly from **assembly** to assembly, and even at times from person to person, and reflects the culture of the people.

Sign of the Cross   The gesture made by touching the tips of the fingers of the right hand to the forehead, mid chest, left shoulder, and right shoulder (or, in the **Byzantine Rite**, the right shoulder before the left shoulder). It is usually accompanied by a spoken Trinitarian formula taken from the baptismal command at the end of Matthew's **Gospel**, "In the name of the Father, and of the Son, and of the Holy Spirit."

Silence   The quiet reflection necessary for prayer. Moments of silence are called for at several times during the celebration of **Mass**: after the invitation to introduce the **penitential act**; after the invitation "Let us pray" before the **collect**; after the **first** and **second readings**; after the **homily**; after the reception of Holy Communion; and after the "Let us pray" before the prayer after communion, unless silence has already been observed after the reception of **Holy Communion**.

Silver   In the dioceses of the United States of America, **vestments** of silver color may be worn at **Mass** in place of **white** vestments on more solemn occasions.

Sing to the Lord: Music in Divine Worship   Document issued by the **United States Conference of Catholic Bishops**, approved in 2007, that deals with music in Catholic **worship**. It addresses music as an integral part of **liturgy**, principles for the selection of appropriate music, and specific questions concerning music in the **rites** of the **Church**. This document replaces the earlier documents *Music in Catholic Worship* and *Liturgical Music Today*.

Skull Cap   A common name for the **zucchetto**.

Solemn Blessing   The form of **blessing** in which the standard Trinitarian formula is usually preceded by three **invocations**. The **assembly** responds to each of these invocations with "**Amen**." Formulas for solemn blessings to be used at **Mass** are given in *The Roman Missal*.

Solemn Intercessions   The **intercessions** prayed at the **Celebration of the Passion of the Lord on Friday of Holy Week (Good Friday)**. The prayers are ancient and ideally follow a format whereby a **deacon** sings or says the invitation in which the intention is announced, all kneel for a period of silent prayer, and then all stand, followed by the **priest** singing or saying the prayer. Ten such intercessions are given in the Missal; the local **bishop** may permit the addition of another intention in the case of grave public need.

Solemnity   A category of liturgical day that is higher than a **feast** or a **memorial**. The celebration of a solemnity begins with **Evening Prayer** I on the preceding day. Some solemnities also have their own **Vigil Mass**, to be used on the evening of the preceding day if Mass is **celebrated** at that time. The two greatest solemnities are **Easter** and the **Nativity of the Lord**, each of which has an **octave**. On solemnities, the **Glory to God in the Highest** and the **Profession of Faith** are prescribed at Mass.

Solesmes   The French Benedictine abbey responsible for the renewal and codification of **Gregorian chant**. It was refounded in 1832 by Dom **Prosper Guéranger**.

Species   One or both of the **consecrated elements** of **bread** and **wine** that have become the Body and Blood of **Christ**. The term is usually *sacred species* when referring to the consecrated elements.

Sponsor   (1) In the Christian initiation of **adults**, one who accompanies a person seeking admission as a catechumen. The sponsor is someone who knows the **candidate** and is able to witness to the candidate's moral character, faith, and intention. He or she accompanies the candidate at the **Rite** of Acceptance into the **order of catechumens** and continues to accompany and support the person through the period of the **catechumenate**.

If the candidate is a **child** of **catechetical age**, it is presumed that the parent will take on this role unless he or she is unable to do so. The sponsor then takes the place of the parent (**RCIA**, 260). The role of sponsor is distinct from that of **godparent**, although the catechumen may choose the sponsor to be the godparent as well.

(2) In the celebration of the **Sacrament** of **Confirmation** with those who were baptized in infancy, one who presents a person being confirmed to the **minister** of the sacrament. After the celebration of the sacrament, the sponsor helps them live in accord with their baptismal promises.

The sponsor for Confirmation is to be a fully initiated member of the Catholic **Church** of sufficient maturity to carry out this role. Paragraph 5 of the *Rite of Confirmation* states a preference that the person's godparent at **Baptism** also serve as the sponsor at Confirmation, but the rite does not exclude the possibility that another person may be chosen.

Stational Mass   A **Mass celebrated** by the **bishop** of the **diocese** with special solemnity on major occasions. At the Stational Mass, the bishop presides, ideally surrounded by his college of **presbyters** and by his **ministers**, and with the full and **active participation** of the faithful. Especially when celebrated in the **cathedral**, this Mass is considered a preeminent manifestation of the local **Church**, showing the unity of the local Church and the diversity of ministries. The 1570 *Roman Missal* indicated an ancient church in Rome for each day during **Lent** at which it was customary for the pope to celebrate a stational Mass. The ancient term *station* was reintroduced in the current *Ceremonial of Bishops*.

Stations of the Cross   A devotional practice that originated when the Franciscans were given custody of the Holy Land in the fourteenth century. In 1731, Pope Clement XII fixed the number at fourteen, and most **churches** erect paintings or sculptures of the designated scenes on the inside walls of the **nave**. The devotion is meant to honor the **Passion** and Death of **Christ**. There are various formats for praying the Stations of the Cross, some of which include a fifteenth station for the Resurrection.

Statues   Three-dimensional images of **art** that provide a focal point for prayer and popular devotion. Although none is required, most **churches** have statues of **Christ**, the Blessed Virgin Mary, St. Joseph, and major patrons.

Stipend   The title, found in the 1917 *Code of Canon Law*, formerly associated with a monetary offering given to a **priest** for celebrating **Mass** for a specific **intention**. The 1983 *Code of Canon Law* uses the word *offering* (*stips*) in place of *stipend* (*stipendium*). According to Thomas Aquinas, *stipend* indicated that the donation was compensation for the time and labor of the priest, since the same word was formerly used to indicate the wage paid to soldiers.

Stock (Holy Oil Stock)   A container in which one of the **holy oils** is kept. The term usually refers to the small metallic vials that are used to carry the oils for use when a **sacrament** is **celebrated** outside the **church**. Decanters or other worthy vessels are used to store and, often, display the holy oils in the **ambry**.

Stole   The **vestment** worn over the neck by ordained **ministers**. It is a long band of fabric about five inches wide. A **priest** or **bishop** wears the stole around the neck and hanging down in front. A **deacon** wears the stole over the left shoulder and fastened at his waist on the right side. At **Mass**, the stole is worn underneath the **chasuble** or **dalmatic**.

Stoup   A container for **holy water** usually found at an entrance to a **church**, also called a holy water **font**. The presence of stoups allows the faithful to bless themselves with water, as a reminder of their **Baptism**, as they enter and leave a church.

Substance   The underlying reality of physical **matter**. It is a classical philosophical term used in distinction to **accidents**. This distinction provides the basis for the explanation of the change in the Eucharistic **elements** in **transubstantiation**.

Summorum Pontificum   Apostolic letter issued *motu proprio* by Pope Benedict XVI on July 7, 2007, giving wider permission for the celebration of **Mass** according to the ***Roman Missal*** promulgated after the **Council of Trent** as updated in 1962 by **Pope John XXIII**, sometimes referred to as the **Tridentine Mass**. It was this document that established the terminology that Mass according to the 1962 Missal is the **extraordinary form of Mass** and that Mass according to the current Missal is the **ordinary form of Mass**.

Sunday   The weekly commemoration of the **Lord's** Resurrection. It is both the first day of the week and also the eighth day. It is also called the **Lord's Day**. Sunday is the original feast day and the preeminent day for the **Church** to gather for **liturgy**.

Sunday Celebrations in the Absence of a Priest   The **ritual** book issued by the **United States Conference of Catholic Bishops' Committee on Divine Worship** in 2007 as a resource for those places in the United States where a **priest** is not available to celebrate the **Eucharist** on a **Sunday**. Such Sunday celebrations, which may include **Holy Communion**, may take the form of a **Liturgy of the Word, Morning Prayer**, or **Evening Prayer**.

Surplice   A white, loose, tunic-like garment worn over a **cassock**. It is derived from the **alb**, and may be worn by **priests** when presiding at non-Eucharistic liturgies. In some parishes **altar servers** vest in cassock and surplice.

Symbol   (1) Something that points beyond itself, triggering an encounter with a deeper reality. In liturgical theology, the symbol, rather than being a mere stand-in for another reality, actually communicates the presence of that which is being symbolized. Therefore, physical realities such as **water** or **bread**, which in themselves sustain life, communicate the presence and action of the deepest reality, the One who creates and sustains all life. Although the word *symbol* is often used interchangeably with *sign*, the two are distinct. A sign merely communicates information with a specific meaning; a symbol reveals transcendent reality and draws one into an encounter with the holy.

(2) A traditional name for the **Profession of Faith**, or **Creed**.

Sympathizer   Another name for an **inquirer**.

Synaxis   A gathering of the faithful for prayer and praise of God. The term is also applied to the **service** that usually occurs after such a gathering takes place. In the **Byzantine Rite**, certain feasts are given the title *synaxis* if they have a special relation to the feast **celebrated** on the previous day, such as the Synaxis of Mary, Mother of God, celebrated on December 26.

T

Tabernacle   The safe-like receptacle for storing the **consecrated** Eucharistic **bread**. When the **Blessed Sacrament** is present in the tabernacle, it is to be locked and the **sanctuary light** alight. The tabernacle must be immovable, solid, and not transparent.

Tabernacle Veil   A **cloth** placed over or in front of the **tabernacle** whenever the **consecrated elements** are stored within. Its use is optional. The **veil** may be **white** or **gold**, though sometimes veils in the various **liturgical colors** are used. Formerly it was called a *conopaeum*.

Table of the Lord   A term sometimes used to refer to the **altar**. Patristic texts also see the **ambo** as being a **symbolic** table, however, and in liturgical writing reference is often made to the "two tables"— i.e., the table of the **Word of God** and the table of the Body of **Christ** (cf. *Constitution on the Sacred Liturgy*, 48, 51).

Te Deum   A **hymn** that begins with the words, "You are God, we praise you." It occurs at the end of the **Office of Readings** on **Sundays** (apart from **Lent**), during the **octaves** of **Easter** and **Christmas**, and on **solemnities** and **feasts**. It is also sung at the end of the **Mass** of the **ordination** of a **bishop** while the new bishop processes through the **assembly** to give his **blessing** and on other joyful occasions.

Temporal Cycle   A term sometimes used to refer to the portion of the **liturgical calendar** related to the liturgical **times** (**Lent, Easter, Advent, Christmas, Ordinary Time**). In contrast, celebrations associated with specific dates, apart from Christmas (such as the Annunciation on March 25), are sometimes called the **sanctoral cycle**.

Thanksgiving   The offering of gratitude to someone, particularly for some benefit received. The celebration of **Mass** is termed **Eucharist**, or thanksgiving, because Christians give thanks to a loving God for salvation and redemption accomplished through the life, Death, and Resurrection of Jesus **Christ**. The motive of thanksgiving finds particular expression in the part of the **Eucharistic Prayer** called the **preface**.

Theodore of Mopsuestia (ca. 350–428)   A fellow student with **John Chrysostom**, he became **Bishop** of Mopsuestia in 392. His *Catecheses* are similar to those of **Cyril of Jerusalem**, but are longer and contain more liturgical texts.

Theophany   A word derived from two Greek words, *Theos* (God) and *phaino* (shine). *Theophany* refers to any manifestation of God, especially of the three Persons of the Trinity together. The **Epiphany** is often called the Theophany in the **Byzantine Rite**, because the **mystery** of **Christ's** **baptism**, at which the Trinity was manifested, is **celebrated**, rather than the visit of the Magi.

Theotokos   The title, meaning "God-bearer," given by the Council of Ephesus in the year 431 to the Blessed Virgin Mary. This Marian title has Christological implications, and is the standard title used of Mary in the Byzantine liturgical texts. It was chosen over Christotokos, or "Christ-bearer," to reflect the **Church's** belief that Mary gave birth not merely to a man who later was united to the divine Word, but to God. The Solemnity of Mary, Mother of God honors Mary as Theotokos.

Three Judgments   Title sometimes given to the process set forth in *Sing to the Lord: Music in Divine Worship* for evaluating the appropriateness of a given piece of music for **liturgy**. The first judgment, the liturgical judgment, determines whether the music meets the demands of the liturgy and supports the liturgical action, thereby conveying the appropriate meaning of the liturgical text or action. Second, the pastoral judgment asks if the selection promotes the active participation of the gathered **assembly** in the **mystery**, and if it is appropriate to the age, culture, language, etc., of the assembly. Finally, the musical judgment ascertains whether it is a good piece of music technically and aesthetically, capable of bearing the weight of mystery.

Thurible   A vessel in which **incense** is burned on coals; also called a **censer**. Originally, thuribles were either open bowls, or **braziers**, that remained stationary or shovel-like containers with handles. Modern thuribles are usually metal vessels with pierced lids that allow air to keep the coals alight. They are suspended by one or more chains and, in the **Roman Rite**, held midway along the chains while swung toward the object or person being reverenced. In the Eastern Rites, the censer is usually swung at the full-length of the chains.

Thurifer   The liturgical **minister** who carries and swings the thurible during liturgies; also called a **censer bearer**. As a ministerial role, it is assigned to an instituted **acolyte** or other **altar server**.

Thurification   Another word for **incensation**.

Thursday of Holy Week   Another name for **Thursday of the Lord's Supper**, or **Holy Thursday**.

Thursday of the Lord's Supper   The liturgical name for **Thursday of Holy Week** after the beginning of the **Paschal Triduum**. The Paschal Triduum begins with the **Evening Mass of the Lord's Supper**. On this day private Masses are forbidden and each community is encouraged to **celebrate** only one Mass.

Time (Liturgical)   A period within the **Church** year, sometimes referred to as a **season**.

The three days of the **Paschal Triduum** are the center point of liturgical time. **Lent** prepares for it, and **Easter Time** extends its celebration. **Advent** prepares for the **Nativity of the Lord**, and **Christmas Time** extends its celebration. **Ordinary Time celebrates** the **mystery** of **Christ** in its fullness, especially on **Sundays**. It occurs in two segments, from the end of Christmas Time until the beginning of Lent, and from the end of Easter Time to the beginning of Advent.

Transept   The sections of a cruciform **church** that extend beyond the main part of the building at right angles, forming the arms of the **cross**.

Transfer of the Body to the Church or to the Place of Committal   One of the **rites** of the *Order of Christian Funerals*. It may be used to pray with the family members and friends of the deceased as they prepare to go to the **church** for the **funeral liturgy** or to the place of committal. The rite includes an invitation, a short Scripture verse, a **litany**, the **Lord's Prayer**, a concluding prayer, and an invitation to the **procession**.

Transubstantiation   The traditional Catholic theological explanation regarding the change of the **bread** and **wine** into the Body and Blood of **Christ** during the celebration of the **Eucharist**. The term is based on the belief that the **substance** of the bread and wine is changed, but the external **accidents** remain unchanged.

Tridentine Rite or Tridentine Mass   The Mass celebrated according to the *Roman Missal* promulgated after the **Council of Trent**, in 1570. It is also a common name for the Mass celebrated according to the 1962 revision of that missal by **Pope John XXIII**, also referred to as the **extraordinary form of the Mass**. Although the **rubrics** for Mass in the 1570 Missal and the 1962 Missal are substantially the same, the 1962 Missal includes revised liturgies for **Holy Week** (from 1955), additional celebrations of **saints** and other feasts, and the inclusion into the **Roman Canon** of the name of St. Joseph.

Triduum Literally, "three days"; another name for the **Paschal Triduum**.

Trisagion An ancient **hymn** to God's holiness, regularly sung in various forms in the Divine **Liturgy**, or **Mass**, of the Eastern **Churches**. The word is Greek for "thrice holy," reflecting the text: "Holy God, Holy and Mighty, Holy and Immortal One, have mercy on us."

Trope A short series of words added to a title or a form of address, in an **invocation**. For example, in the third form of the **penitential act**, in the invocation, "You were sent to heal the contrite of heart: Lord have mercy," the phrase "You were sent to heal the contrite of heart" is a trope.

Turner, Victor (1920–1983) Anthropologist who specialized in comparative religions, particularly the use of **rituals** and **symbols**. He introduced the theory of liminality in his book *The Ritual Process* as a way of describing religious **rites** as threshold experiences.

Typical Edition The original version of a **ritual** book published in **Latin** under the auspices of the **Congregation for Divine Worship and the Discipline of the Sacraments**. It is from this Latin typical edition (*editio typica*) that translations into the **vernacular** are to be made.

U

United States Conference of Catholic Bishops (USCCB)
An assembly of the **hierarchy** of the United States (and the US Virgin Islands) who jointly exercise certain pastoral functions in order to promote Catholic activities in the United States through various apostolates. Among the various departments that carry out the work of the Conference is the **Committee on Divine Worship**.

Universal Norms on the Liturgical Year and the General Roman Calendar The document that outlines the regulations governing the celebrations of the **liturgical year** and the calendar for the universal **Church**. The liturgical days, their ranking, and the cycle of the year are all explained, and a table of liturgical days ranks the order of importance of the liturgical celebrations of the Church. It was promulgated by **Pope Paul VI** in 1969.

Universal Prayer The intercessory prayers in the celebration of the **Mass**, following the **Creed** on **Sundays** and **solemnities** or the **homily** on other days; also called the **Prayer of the Faithful** or **Bidding Prayers**, and formerly called the General **Intercessions**. It consists of an introduction, **intentions** and **responses** to the intentions, and a concluding prayer.

Usher The liturgical **minister** who helps seat people as they arrive at the **church** for **worship**, who takes up the **collection**, and who helps organize and direct **processions** of the faithful, such as the **procession with the gifts** and the communion procession. An usher may also fulfill the ministry of **greeter**.

V

Veil In liturgical usage, a cloth worn over the shoulders or used to cover a liturgical object. Various veils are used in the course of liturgies. The **chalice** may be covered with a veil when not in use. A **priest** or **deacon** wears a **humeral veil** when carrying the **Blessed Sacrament** in **procession**. A **minister** assisting a **bishop** may wear a light veil, called a **vimpa**, when holding the **miter** or **crosier**. During the two weeks before **Easter**, **statues** and **crosses** may be veiled in **violet**. The Showing of the Holy Cross may begin with a veiled cross during the **Celebration of the Passion of the Lord on Good Friday**. A **tabernacle veil** may be used to indicate the presence of the **Eucharist**.

Vernacular The language commonly used by people in a given geographical area.

Verse before the Gospel The **acclamation** sung before the **Gospel** during **Lent** that takes the place of the **Alleluia**, which is not used from **Ash Wednesday** until the **Easter Vigil** in the **Roman Rite**. It normally consists of a refrain addressed to **Christ** sung by all, and an intervening verse, usually scriptural.

Versus Populum **Latin** for "facing the people," the celebration of **Mass** in which the **priest** faces the people. This posture was restored in the liturgical reforms of the Second Vatican Council for all the reformed **rites**.

Vespers Another name for **Evening Prayer**, one of the **offices** of the **Liturgy of the Hours**.

Vestibule   The anteroom of a **church**, between the entrance and the **nave**. A large vestibule is ofte n called a **narthex** or **gathering place**.

Vesting Room   The room where the liturgical **vestments** are stored and where **ministers** for **liturgy** vest; also called the **secretarium**.

Vestments   The **ritual** garments and **symbols** of **office** worn by various **ministers** at **liturgy**. The vestment for all ministers in the **sanctuary** is the **alb**, over which ordained ministers add a **stole**. At the celebration of the **Eucharist**, **bishops** and **priests** wear a **chasuble** over the alb and stole, and a **deacon** wears a **dalmatic**. The **cope**, a long, cape-like vestment is worn by ordained ministers over an alb and stole for solemn liturgies outside **Mass**. Copes may also be worn for solemn **processions**.

Vesture   A general term for **vestments**.

Viaticum   Latin for "provisions for a journey." Viaticum is **Holy Communion** received before death as food and nourishment for the journey to heaven; it may be **celebrated** within or outside Mass. The **rite** for the giving of communion as viaticum also gives the sick person the opportunity to renew his or her baptismal profession of faith. Viaticum is the last **sacrament**, administered after the **Anointing of the Sick**.

Vigil   A **service** held on the evening prior to the actual day. The greatest and most noble vigil is the **Easter Vigil**. Certain **solemnities** have their own Vigil **Mass**, i.e.—**Epiphany**, **Pentecost**, the Nativity of St. John the Baptist, the Assumption of the Blessed Virgin Mary, and the Nativity of the **Lord**.

Vigil for the Deceased   One of the **rites** in the *Order of Christian Funerals*. Sometimes called a wake **service**, the Vigil for the Deceased is the principal service following death and before the **funeral liturgy**. It may be **celebrated** in the home of the deceased, in the funeral home or **chapel** of rest, or in the parish **church**. At this **liturgy**, the community keeps watch with the family, finding strength in **Christ's** presence. The structure is that of a service of the word. The rite may be led by a **priest, deacon,** or **lay minister**.

Vimpa   A **veil** that may be worn by the **miter bearer** and **crosier bearer** at a **Mass celebrated** by a **bishop**. A vimpa is similar to the **humeral veil** but narrower, of lighter fabric, and more simply adorned. The ends of the vimpa should be wrapped around the **miter** and **crosier** while they are being held, to prevent them from becoming soiled.

Violet   The **color** used during **Advent** and **Lent**. It may also be used in **Offices** and **Masses for the Dead**.

Votive Candles   Small **candles** placed before **altars**, shrines, or **statues** and lit by the faithful as a sign of their prayers.

Votive Masses   A selection of **Masses** found in *The Roman Missal* that may be **celebrated** at the wish (in **Latin**, *votum*) of the presiding **priest** for pastoral benefit. The texts used are not those of the current liturgical **time** or day; rather they honor God, Mary, the **angels**, and the **saints**. Masses in the **Proper** of Saints may also be used as Votive Masses, within limitations (GIRM, 375). Liturgical norms regulate when Votive Masses may be used (GIRM, 376).

Washing of Feet   The **rite** imitating the **Lord's** act of washing his disciples' feet at the **Last Supper**. It may take place in the **Roman Rite** after the **homily** at the **Evening Mass of the Lord's Supper** on **Holy Thursday**. It is also called the **Mandatum**. In the writings of St. Ambrose of Milan, a washing of feet of the newly baptized is mentioned in connection with the baptismal **liturgy**.

Washing of Hands   The **ritual** cleansing that takes place during the **preparation of the gifts**, sometimes called the **lavabo**. Originally a practical action necessary because the **celebrant** handled a variety of foodstuffs in receiving the gifts of the **assembly**, it is now a gesture of the desire for interior purification.

Water   An abundant gift of God's creation, vital for all known forms of life. It is used in Christian **worship** in many ways, most importantly in the **Sacrament of Baptism**, a washing that symbolizes plunging into the Death of **Christ** and rising with him to new life. Water is used as a reminder of **Baptism**, as when people enter or leave the **church**, or are sprinkled with it during **Mass**. Water, representing Christ's humanity, is mixed into **wine** before **consecration**. Water is also used by the **priest** to **wash his hands** during the **preparation of the gifts**.

White   The **liturgical color** used during **Easter Time** and **Christmas Time**, on celebrations of the **Lord** other than his **Passion**, on celebrations of the Blessed Virgin Mary, **angels**, and **saints** who were not **martyrs**, and on many **solemnities**. It is also the color of the garment given to the newly baptized (see **white garment**).

White Garment   The clothing, often similar to an **alb**, which is given to someone immediately after **Baptism**. This garment is a **sign** that the newly baptized person has put on new life in **Christ**. It is used in the Baptism of both **adults** and **children**.

Whitsunday   The name used in the United Kingdom and Ireland for **Pentecost**.

Wine   Grape wine without additives, either red or white, is used at **Mass**. A small amount of **water** is mixed with the wine when the **chalice** is prepared before the **Eucharistic Prayer**.

Word of God   Another name for the **Bible**. Jesus is also referred to as the Word of God.

Words of Institution   Another name for the **Institution Narrative**.

Worship   Our expression of love, reverence, honor, and adoration of a good and gracious God through various communal and private activities. In Christian tradition, the worshipping **assembly** generally prays to God the Father through **Christ**, in the unity of the Holy Spirit. Expressions of public worship are not usually directed to Christ, although exceptions, particularly the **Kyrie** and the **Agnus Dei**, exist in the Mass. In both these cases, it is the assembly that addresses Christ in prayer, while the presiding **priest** normally prays to God the Father, as in the **Eucharistic Prayer**. Even to this there are exceptions, such as the prayer the **presider** says before the **sign of peace** ("**Lord** Jesus Christ, who said to your Apostles . . . ") or the **collect** for the morning Mass on December 24, which begins, "Come quickly, we pray, Lord Jesus, and do not delay."

Z

Zikkaron   The Hebrew word for active remembering, corresponding to the Greek word *anamnesis*.

Zucchetto   A **skull cap**. It is usually worn by those who have the right to wear a **miter**, such as **bishops** and abbots. It is also worn by members of certain religious **orders** in some countries. A bishop's zucchetto is purple in color; a cardinal's is red; the pope's is white. It is also called by the **Latin** word *pileolus*.

About the Authors

Dennis C. Smolarski, SJ, is a Jesuit priest and professor of mathematics and computer science at Santa Clara University. He is the author of several books on liturgy, including *Q&A: Seasons, Sacraments, and Sacramentals*; *Q&A: The Mass* (both from LTP); and *Eucharist and American Culture: Liturgy, Unity, and Individualism* (Paulist, 2010), as well as several works on math and computers. He holds master of divinity and master of sacred theology degrees from the Jesuit School of Theology at Berkeley and a PHD in computer science from the University of Illinois.

Joseph DeGrocco, a priest of the Diocese of Rockville Centre, is pastor of Our Lady of Perpetual Help Church in Lindenhurst, New York. He is the author of several works, including *A Pastoral Commentary on the General Instruction of the Roman Missal* and *Guide for Celebrating Funerals,* from Liturgy Training Publications. He holds a master of arts degree in theology (liturgical studies) from the University of Notre Dame and a doctorate in ministry from the Seminary of the Immaculate Conception, where he also serves as professor of liturgy.